# OUR LADY

# OF

# HOT MESSES

"In a culture obsessed with social media–perfect posts, Leticia Ochoa Adams's voice is a needed breath of fresh air. Her raw and honest story is a reminder that all people, regardless of their past or trauma, are loved by God even in the messiness."

**Alessandra Harris**
Writer and author of *Last Place Seen*

"God bless this mess! Funny, engaging, haunting, and real— this is the book a growing Church needs. Ready or not, you're gon' learn today!"

**Marcia Lane-McGee**
Coauthor of *Fat Luther, Slim Pickin's*

"There is nothing more powerful and yet nothing that makes one more vulnerable than sharing a personal testimony. I was moved to tears and driven to see the Lord on my knees as I heard Leticia Ochoa Adams's heart and its cry for answers. Through trial, loss, and pain she held on to the Hope Giver, who gave her hope and consolation. Wow! I cannot recommend *Our Lady of Hot Messes* enough. You will laugh, cry, and be drawn to God through every page. Thank you, Leticia Ochoa Adams, for your brutal honesty and for bringing hope to those who are struggling to find it."

**Fr. Rob Galea**
Author of *Breakthrough*

# OUR LADY OF HOT MESSES

## Getting Real with God in Dive Bars and Confessionals

### LETICIA OCHOA ADAMS

AVE MARIA PRESS AVE Notre Dame, Indiana

Scripture quotations are from *New Revised Standard Version Bible*, copyright ©
1989 National Council of the Churches of Christ in the United States of
America. Used by permission. All rights reserved worldwide.

Foreword © 2022 by Nora McInerny

_____

© 2022 by Leticia Ochoa Adams

Founded in 1865, Ave Maria Press is a ministry of the United States Province
of Holy Cross.

www.avemariapress.com

Paperback: ISBN-13 978-1-64680-150-3

E-book: ISBN-13 978-1-64680-151-0

Cover image © 2020 Universal Images Group Editorial.

Cover and text design by Samantha Watson.

Printed and bound in the United States of America.

*Library of Congress Cataloging-in-Publication Data is available.*

To my four children,
Anthony, Dan, Gabe, and Oli:
y'all deserved better.

To my grandchildren,
Aaliyah and Cammie,
and their mother, Ariana:
thank you for being
my hype humans.

# CONTENTS

# FOREWORD
## BY NORA MCINERNY

I grew up as one link in a long chain of proud Irish Catholics, so you'd think I'd understand the concept of confession long before the date of my First Confession arrived.
You'd be wrong. I was a second grader at Annunciation
Catholic Church in South Minneapolis, and my class had
been preparing for this milestone for weeks. I knew what I
was expected to do: go into the confessional and, you know,
confess. Instead, I stepped into the cool dark of the confessional and told the priest that I had nothing to confess to. In
all eight years of my life, I had yet to commit a single, soli-
tary sin. Befuddled, Fr. Ken offered some thought starters:
Perhaps I'd disobeyed my parents? *No, not really.* Had I been
mean to my brother? *Only when he started it.* Father pushed,
and I pushed back. Why should I apologize for being a kid?
If this was going to be my First Confession, I wanted it to
be good—maybe I should have swiped a few bucks from
the collection plate beforehand? Fr. Ken and I ended my
First Confession agreeing to disagree, but I realized afterward that everyone else in my class had truly understood

the assignment and had come out of the confessional with homework. I mean, I guess *technically* it was penances, but still, I felt embarrassed, stupid, and scared: Would Fr. Ken call my parents and let them know I'd failed my confession? To his credit, he did not. (Thanks for that, Father!)

Here is a confession that will not surprise you: I have not always had a great relationship with God. I wanted to, but I didn't know how to get it right. I mean, I couldn't even get my *confession* correct! Surely, God would be more focused on the kids who copped to having pinched their brother until he gave up the remote control, the people who didn't have so many questions, the ones who woke up in time for Sunday Mass without complaining. And while we're on the topic of confessing, I'm not sure I even count as a Catholic anymore. I haven't been to confession since that first round with Fr. Ken, I never give anything up for Lent, and I've questioned my belonging in a faith that I didn't choose and that seems at times, ya know, a little judgy.

A lot of people find their faith in tragedy, but after losing a pregnancy, my very Catholic father, and my husband in the fall of 2014, I felt further from God than I ever had. Prayer felt like talking to a blank wall. Stepping into church felt like waiting on the dentist. I was jealous of people with faith. I wanted what they had, and I didn't know how to get it. It was official: God and I were broken up. Fine, no big deal, I'd gotten through plenty of breakups in my life, what was one more? The world was a hard place, and it was clear to me that down here, we were on our own.

And then I met Leticia Ochoa Adams. If you're a person who has been through something—or is going through something—you know when you meet a fellow traveler on this rough road. Within two minutes of meeting Leticia, I knew what her thing was: she'd lost her firstborn son, Anthony, to suicide. We hugged, we cried, and we followed each other on Instagram. A friendship was born, and I learned that Anthony wasn't the only sorrow that Leticia was carrying: she'd spent a lifetime surviving a series of traumas from childhood sexual abuse to domestic violence. What we survived was different, but *how* we survived it was the same: dark humor and lots of swearing. Our stories were hard for people to hear, but we told them anyway, and we found communities of people who needed to know that they weren't alone.

What Leticia had that I didn't was faith: while I was raised a Catholic, she had found the Church as an adult, and I was shocked. *Catholic women can swear, listen to rap, and smoke cigarettes?* I thought. *Maybe if someone had told me that I would have stuck around!* Leticia was different from the kind of Catholic I had known most of my life. Her faith wasn't a blunt object meant to force someone to conform to her beliefs or a warm fuzzy blanket to cover up their open wounds. It was an exploration, an examination, a way of seeing the world with curiosity and acceptance. The more we spoke, the more I realized we saw eye to eye on nearly everything, even though I'm a foot taller than her. (Bad joke, sorry.) Leticia's faith has made me feel closer to God, and Catholicism, than I ever did in a lifetime of Catholic school and weekly Mass.

Because this book isn't just a Catholic story; this is a life story. Because no matter what you believe, your world is subject to change without notice (and truly, it never gives notice). This is a book for those of us who have struggled to feel worthy of a relationship with God, who have felt like our pasts would make it impossible to cross the threshold of a church without bursting into flames. It's a book for those of us holding onto a pain so sharp and so heavy that religion seems like the very last thing on earth that would possibly help. It's a book for people who *know* God loves them but think, *Maybe God just has bad taste.* In her stories of suffering and survival, Leticia introduces us to the God I wish I'd been able to see when I was deep in my own suffering: a God who sticks around, even when we don't think we're worthy, even when we feel forgotten, even when—as Leticia did—you bring your kid to work with you at Hooter's. The world is filled with people who will tell you who and how to be, but here you will find that your messy self *is* your best self.

In the years since that first confession with Fr. Ken, I *have* learned how to confess, and I've also learned that there are plenty of people like me, like Leticia, like you. We might be hot messes, but as Leticia says, God loves us anyway.

# INTRODUCTION

Life is so crazy. I used to think that I was doing it all wrong, that because I hadn't figured out the secret code that everyone else seemed to know, God was not interested in helping me with my life. I grew up going to a First Baptist Church in a small, rural south Texas town. I was a good little Baptist girl until I met a boy who looked just like Donnie Wahlberg, who French-kissed me on the steps of that same First Baptist Church. At that point I left behind both my King James Bible that I received when I was eight years old and the idea that if I answered enough altar calls I would be normal.

God went his way, and I went mine.

Starting about then, my life took a lot of twists and turns. I acted out in reaction to the trauma of being sexually abused as a child. I met my first husband (not the boy on the church steps) and married him two weeks after our first date. He instantly became a father to the three-year-old son I already had. We had a late-term miscarriage a few months later and then three kids back-to-back right away. He began struggling with drug addiction, which led to us getting a divorce eight years after our whirlwind marriage.

No matter what, I seemed to never be able to unlock the life code, so I turned to the person that every American woman turns to when looking for a way to make a better life for herself: Oprah.

My whole life I knew what I wanted. I wanted a family. I wanted a husband, kids, a nice house, and a good life where I didn't have to buy groceries with food stamps or worry about how to pay the light bill. I wanted a car that I could afford and that would not leave me stranded on the highway. I wanted to feel safe and provide that feeling of safety for others. But how? Now that I was divorced, I had no clue, but I figured that Oprah might help.

And in a way, she did. I learned about child sex abuse and the language that allowed me to finally explain what had happened to me without blaming anyone but the person who hurt me. It would be years before I walked into a therapist's office to do the hard work of processing the trauma that had been a part of my life since age five, when a man molested and raped me for the first time, but learning these words from Oprah helped me to express my pain and my hurt.

I eventually began therapy because the same boy who French-kissed me at the First Baptist Church in Kenedy, Texas, ended up marrying me in 2010 after my conversion to Catholicism. I had actually been Catholic all my life, despite attending the First Baptist Church, because I had been baptized Catholic as a baby. I also checked the "Catholic" box every time I was arrested, but that was it. In every other respect, I thought Catholics were nuts, and I wanted nothing to do with being Catholic. But in a Hail Mary effort to get

Stacey to marry me when we were living together, I began the Rite of Christian Initiation of Adults (RCIA). My only goal was for him to marry me. God had other plans.

During a trip to Rome, God wooed me. Or duped me, depending on how you look at it. I came into the Church during the Easter Vigil of 2010. My four children were baptized, confirmed, and received their First Holy Communion as well. The following October, Stacey and I were married in the Catholic Church. The next year my three stepchildren also received the rest of their sacraments.

We lived happily ever after.

Ha! No, we didn't. The years to come were full of mistakes, tears, and so many fights. Once again, I felt as if I was failing somehow. Failing to be a good Christian. Somewhere in my mind, I felt that if God loved me, then we would not be suffering the things we were suffering. But the truth is that suffering is a part of the human condition. Trauma does not go away when you are confirmed. What God does promise us is that he will be with us through all of it. Despite all the work I had done in starting therapy, attending RCIA, and more, I did not believe that truth for a very long time, and then the worst happened.

In March of 2017, my oldest son, Anthony, died by suicide. This was the first time in my life that I questioned whether God existed. The next few years were hard, and I struggled with my faith. I was wrestling with God every moment of the day. I was angry, hurt, and heartbroken. Through all that, God and I grew closer than ever. Not because he made it all better. This will never be better.

Anthony is dead, but God is still God. Learning to trust God with the soul of my child taught me how to trust him with everything. Including my grief. Including my past. I did not have to be OK; I just had to be me.

I began looking back at all the lessons I had learned and the experiences I had had that were signs of God's love for me, and they looked different than anything I had read any Christian talk about. Like sitting on a barstool for years playing Peter Gabriel's song "In Your Eyes" as a prayer. Or using the quiet time in the mornings when I worked at Hooters to talk to God about the dreams I had for my children as I sliced lemons.

I have spent the last four years learning who God is rather than who I have always thought he was. I have learned that he has always been with me, even when I was dancing on speakers at a club. I want to pass on some of those lessons to anyone who thinks, like I used to, that they are beyond the reach of God's love. The second time I sat in RCIA, a man named Noe Rocha told me that God loves me more than I think he does. That changed the direction of my life. So here I am, telling you the same thing.

God loves you more than you think he does. No matter what you have done or how far you have gone, he is waiting for you to come back to him.

After all, he did the same for me.

# 1.
# JESUS IS NOT YOUR BFF

This is not an easy chapter for me to write because I was raised Baptist. Well, I raised myself Baptist. It began when my mom owned a daycare and babysat two girls whose mom offered to take me to Vacation Bible School one summer. In my mind, it was magical. The people were so nice, there were snacks, and we learned about Jesus as this guy that loved me more than anything. He was my friend.

In the background of learning about Jesus, I was being sexually abused at home. The abuse began around the age of five, and it stopped when I was nine and started my period. While I don't have clear memories of most of what I experienced, both the clear and foggy memories are enough to make my breath stop as I type this.

Needless to say, as a child enduring that horror, I was looking for a savior. I can now say that what I was looking for in that savior was safety. My mom, who also had a difficult childhood, did the best she could as a single mother to keep me safe. It was her priority, and we butted heads on it a lot of times, but as a middle-aged mother and grandmother, I now appreciate that my mother was always looking out for what was best for me. But I also know that we cannot always keep bad things from happening to our kids, no matter how much we try. The Jesus I was told about at Vacation Bible School was exactly the savior that I was looking for. A God who would die for me, love me, and take down my enemies while granting all my wishes. He was going to give me a dad and make my mom happy. He was going to make me behave. And man, everything about me that was inappropriate? Jesus was going to fix all that.

But he did not. After answering every altar call from the ages of eleven to thirteen, and I mean *every* one, I found that I still could not say yes when asked whether I was in a personal relationship with Jesus. I felt that if I did have that kind of relationship with him, I would not be so "bad." And that is how I felt about myself, that I was bad and I needed a miracle to be good. I answered so many altar calls trying to get Jesus to "live in my heart" that the Baptists did the only thing they could think of: they baptized me twice. I have gone through the ritual many times—as a Catholic when I was a baby, and then twice as a Baptist, and once by Pentecostals. No amount of dunking and baptizing could fix me.

When I was twelve years old, I was standing by my best friend's locker when the hottest boy I had ever seen walked down the hall. He was the new kid on the block and looked just like Donnie Walhberg. I loved Stacey from the moment I first saw him. I wrote him love notes telling him he was going to marry me. He did not believe me. He was a young, stupid teenage boy, and I was pretty much an outcast by that point. I was desperate for someone to love me and save me. I was an open target for bullying and people making fun of me. I was the most pitiful teen girl. Which meant that even though Stacey and I would find any moment to make out at the First Baptist Church in front of his house (God is good), he never wanted anyone to think that he was my boyfriend. That really hurt me. I felt like the loser I always felt like, but I kept making out with him because he was so cute and I loved him. We made plans to have sex for the first time, which would have happened except for the fact that I asked him if he would marry me and have kids with me if we did it. That stopped that entire situation pretty freakin' fast.

Everything we did up to that point, though, triggered me. I realized that I had done all of this before, and the flashbacks of what had happened to me as a child, memories that I had repressed and now had to face as if they had just happened, came back to me. Then, two days after the failed sex attempt, Stacey broke up with me and began dating my best friend. The triggers from my abuse, the betrayal of my friend, and the reality that Stacey did not love me created the perfect storm. I began to run away for days at a time. I started sneaking out of the house and sleeping with a man in his twenties. Within months, I had slept with half a dozen guys, some of them adults and some my age, all of them benefiting from my desperate need to be loved. The only way that I had been taught to be loved was to let someone use my body.

I could not understand why nobody loved me. We were told at the First Baptist Church that if Jesus lived in our hearts, then we would not have sex outside of marriage, so it seemed to me that even Jesus didn't want to love me. The chastity talks I heard at youth group told us that girls who have sex are used gum but did not tell us that boys who use girls are assholes. It was not a good message for anyone, let alone a young girl who had been groomed and sexually abused as a child. It is not easy to explain all the internal messages that you end up with after that happens to you at such a young age. It wasn't something I knew how to vocalize to anyone, but the messages I was getting about chastity only made me more confused, not more chaste.

At fourteen I decided that if I was used gum, I was just going to go my way. I was not going to be an atheist, but I was not going to church anymore. Jesus had made it clear that he was not OK with me; after all, I had gotten nothing that I wished for. My confused idea of sex, the abuse I had suffered as a child, and my belief that Jesus was not my best friend but was still God all created this illusion that I was not good enough to be in church. And so I left.

The last time I ran away I spent days in a mobile home with a boy. We had sex the entire time with the Eagles playing on a loop. To this day, I refuse to live in a mobile home ever or listen to that Eagles album. This boy did not hurt me or manipulate me, but he did use me. He got off on having me do whatever he asked. All I wanted was someone to be nice to me. When he was done with me, he sent me home. And I had to walk. I cried as I walked down the highway because I did not understand why, after everything I had done to get that boy to love me, he had sent me away like nothing. A high school boy who lived along that highway saw me and told me I could use his phone to call someone to get me. I followed him, and before I knew it, I was in a barn bent over a bale of hay being raped instead of on the phone getting a ride. He said that I could tell anyone I wanted but nobody would believe me because everyone knew how easy I was. He was not wrong.

That was what broke me. I got back on the highway, and I just wanted to disappear. I did not see any way forward in my life. At the moment when I was at my most hopeless, a truck pulled up behind me. When I looked back, it was my Tio Roy. I looked awful after days of not eating or showering. There was nobody I wanted to see less than that man. He was the father I never had, and I was terrified of disappointing him. But as much as I didn't want him to see me like that, I also did not have the guts to run away. I jumped in his truck, and he asked, "What the hell is wrong with you? Why are you doing this?" I just told him everything. From start to finish without leaving anything out. About what happened to me as a child, how Jesus did not live in my heart, and everything with Stacey. I even told him about what had happened in the barn right before he found me. Before I knew it, we were pulling up to his house. He told me to go in and let my Tia know that I was staying with them.

My Tia Mary told me to take a bath, and she gave me something to wear from one of my oldest cousins. She fed me, and I went to sleep. When I woke up, all my things were there, and the next day I was enrolled in a new school. Years later, I would hear that my Tio showed up at my house with his shotgun and said that he was taking me and my things and told the man who had abused me that if he ever came near me again that he would regret it. For once in my life, someone kept me safe. When I was grown and my Tio was dying, all I kept thinking was that I was losing my hero. I am so lucky that when he was first diagnosed with prostate cancer, I was able to write him a letter telling him how he saved me and how much I loved him. My gift of writing gave me the ability to express to him how much he meant to me.

Not long after I moved in with my Tio Roy and Tia Mary, my mom left our house and came to get me. Eventually we ended up in Amarillo, Texas, which was very far from Three Rivers, where I had grown up. I did not want to move at all. Within a year, at only sixteen, I was pregnant with my oldest son. When he was almost three years old, I married my first husband, had a miscarriage, and then quickly birthed three more kids. When Ben and I got divorced, I moved to Austin. In 2008, I received a message from none other than Stacey Adams. He was in Iraq and was also divorced. I had just caught Ben doing drugs again, so even though we were divorced, this time our relationship was really over.

When Stacey came home, we moved to the Austin suburbs in July of 2008. I wanted him to marry me, so I began RCIA, the Rite of Christian Initiation of Adults—the same move I made when I was pregnant with Anthony. I never had any intention of actually becoming Catholic; I just wanted to marry my childhood sweetheart. God is hilarious. This RCIA class was taught by a man named Noe Rocha. I thought he was nice enough, but I was sure that nothing bad had ever happened to him because he worked for the Church and church people, in my experience, had everything good. Turned out that Noe used to be addicted to heroin. And on top of that, he had had plenty of bad things happen to him. He also talked about Jesus like he knew him. I wanted that. And that was when God hooked me.

Throughout my conversion, I encountered a different Jesus than the one preached in my childhood. Jesus was not fluffy. He called out Pharisees. He spoke frankly. He was not this best friend kind of softy that I had thought he was. He talked about hell—not in a threatening way, but in a way that was realistic. We have choices and those choices have consequences; some consequences are eternal. That was the hell Jesus talked about. With my past, I had to find the balance between what was done to me and what I could do to process it and heal from it, because being angry and bitter was not helping me or my children at all. Holding on to all that pain was killing me. God understands what trauma is and how we make choices out of those wounds, but he also gives us tools to help heal us.

Having my Tio and Tia in my life set me up very well to understand how God could be both merciful and just. It is not one or the other but both at the same time. When I was stopped for driving while intoxicated in 2007, my Tio and Tia were both there for me. But both of them expected me to get my act together. Both of them held me accountable for my actions while also making it clear to me that they would always love me. I tried to do the same thing for my children, and when I converted to Catholicism, it was easy for me to understand that God has rules. They were not rules for the sake of controlling me, but rules to keep me safe. My entire life I had been seeking that kind of safety while making choices that hurt me because I did not understand how the rules kept me safe. In the same way, I did not understand that my mother was trying to keep me safe by telling me not to do things that she knew would hurt me. I thought she was being mean and unfair when, really, she was just trying to protect me. Once I realized that the "rules" are not rules at all but are God's way of saying, "This will hurt you," I came to understand that the safety I had been seeking all my life was right in front of me. No human being can give it to me; it only comes in trusting God and believing that he does in fact love me and want good things for me.

Because I now have this understanding that God will never not love me, I can show up in prayer honestly with Jesus. I am safe to be myself and be honest with him. Jesus gets my sense of humor; he gets why I do not think cussing is as big of a deal as someone else does; and he delights in me, not because I am like this person or that person but because I am me and he loves me just as I am.

Jesus is so much more than a best friend. He is Love and Justice and Mercy. Everything he is is ordered to justice. Trusting in that is how I forgive the man who abused me and how I trust God with Anthony's soul. Because I know that in the end, I am safe.

# 2.
# SHEEP ARE DUMB

When I was coming into the Church, one day my favorite priest was talking to the kids about Jesus as the Good Shepherd. He said that the Bible calls us sheep so often because sheep are dumb. Jesus knew this. Sheep wander off and get lost, they are eaten by predators, and they need to be protected. It is the love of a shepherd that keeps them safe and sound. A lot of modern-day shepherds also use guard dogs who live with the sheep and keep them safe from predators. I think of our guardian angels as sort of like God's guard dogs.

After hearing Fr. J talk about sheep and how they are so dumb, I became obsessed. I badly wanted to see a herd of sheep, but not just any herd of sheep: I wanted to see a herd that had a shepherd. I live in central Texas, and when I first heard that story, I lived in the suburbs. The lack of herds of sheep led by shepherds was real.

In March of 2010, when Stacey and I were living together, we tried to elope in Rome as if it was the Catholic Vegas. Spoiler: it is not Catholic Vegas, especially during

Lent, which is when we were visiting. The guy behind the
window of the marriage license office almost fell out of his
chair when we said we wanted to get married but we didn't
have a letter from a priest and, even worse, I did not have
any of my sacraments other than Baptism. He thought it
was a great joke. We were such bad Catholics that we didn't
get the punch line.

On our last day in Rome we went for a walk by our hotel,
which was located on the outskirts of the city. We did not
want to stay in the touristy part of Rome, so we had picked
a hotel that was nestled in a neighborhood. On our last full
day there, we decided to go on an adventure walking around
the Roman countryside. We left the main street and ended
up passing fields, including one that had a cute donkey that
let us pet him. Soon we were on a cobblestone road walking
past Romans on their own crisp Sunday stroll. It was the
most gorgeous day.

As we were walking down the road, I saw a cloud of
white moving off to the side and wondered aloud what it
could be. As we got closer, the cloud came into focus, and
soon I could see that it was a flock of sheep heading right
toward us. Before we could register what was happening,
we were surrounded by white sheep. Big sheep and little
sheep, followed closely by a really old shepherd. He looked
like he had come out of a time machine with his satchel
and wooden staff. The sheep were jumping around, playing
with each other, and there was something about them that
made me freeze in amazement. When I saw the smirk on the
shepherd's face, I realized that it looked familiar: it was the

same expression Jesus had in the picture at my parish ..... that seemed to follow me around the adoration chapel. When the shepherd and I locked eyes, I could feel God telling me, "See how much I love you? You asked for a real-life example of a herd of sheep with their shepherd, and here you go. There is nothing I will not do for you."

At that moment I decided I was going to *be* Catholic. I wasn't just going to join the Church to get my boyfriend to marry me, but I would actually be Catholic. I would learn all of the teachings of the Church and follow them, even if they seemed insane. And a lot of them did seem insane to me. Some of them still do, but the one thing that moment showed me is that by following the voice of Jesus, the Good Shepherd, I am safe. I am free to play and walk and do my sheep thing because he keeps me safe.

Safety is the one thing that I had been looking for my entire life, and I did not even know it. It took me a decade in therapy before I could express that need to be safe and admit to myself that I had never been safe in my life. It was not until that walk in Rome that I even saw what safety looked like. It looked like a shepherd smirking while his stupid sheep jumped around with joy.

Just like sheep, we are stupid. We look for comfort, thinking it is the same as safety, but comfort can be a trap. It lulls us into a trance where we lose our instincts—our sense of when things are wrong or need to change—and we lose our relationships with each other because we stop working to maintain them. More important, we lose our relationship with God.

In June of 2021, my husband and I moved out to ten acres of raw land, which means that we moved an RV onto a pasture that still had fresh cow patties on it and lived there. The entire move was emotional and scary. On our first night on the land, there was a bad thunderstorm that almost killed us. The area where we were parked flooded, and a tree just feet away from the RV was struck by lightning. The dogs were so scared that all three of them were sitting on me; I was so scared that I let them. Since that night, there have been many other scary moments. More storms, flooding, getting stuck in the mud, generators going down, hot-water heaters leaking, and moments when I was sure that we were all going to die. But in that fear, I have trusted God's love for me more than I ever have in my life because it is the only option. Either he loves me and, even if I die, I will be OK, or he does not exist and then how all this rolling thunder came to be really makes no sense. Nothing makes you believe in God more than being in the middle of raw land when lightning strikes. Only God could make something that powerful happen.

And that is the greatest lesson I have learned since we moved—how much we are connected to God and how comfort numbs us from knowing that. On the land, we have to be alert to everything: the weather, the danger of the grass catching fire, the amount of food we can store in a small RV fridge, the best way to cook in order to save on propane. We have to think intentionally about how we will feed ourselves, including planning to raise beef cows, get a dairy cow, and raise chickens for their eggs and meat. All of these things have increased my awareness of our relationship with our land, animals, home, and food, and have also caused my relationship with God to grow.

God gave us everything we need to live and thrive: animals, vegetables, the ability to grow and harvest them, and the senses and intelligence to understand the moon, clouds, and weather patterns. Being aware of all these things means living in the present moment as it is, rather than how we might wish it to be. It means working hard and engaging all of our senses in the here and now.

I am a dumb sheep who thought that binge-watching Netflix while I waited for Uber Eats to deliver my McDonald's was living my best life, but really that was me living a numb and zoned-out life. I was miserable, but I didn't know why. I was unfulfilled and unsatisfied. There are still days when I am those things, but then I pet my bunnies, cut some grass, or feel the earth under my feet as I watch the deer tend to their fawns or a cottontail run across the field in front of me, and I come back to my body.

I feel more and more healed with each sunset. On these ten acres, I feel nestled in the chest of my Shepherd. I feel safe. This way of life has healed me in the places that therapy could not reach.

A few weeks ago, I stopped to pick up some pasture-raised beef from a couple selling it in the small town nearby. We were talking about raising meat animals, and I told them we had ten acres on the other side of town. The husband said, "Well, let me just tell you, do not get sheep. We had sheep and we left them loose on the land and each one was killed by something." This made me think about Fr. J's words about how dumb sheep are. Jesus knew exactly what he meant when he labeled us sheep. We need to be protected, or we will be drawn away from the places where we are safe and killed one by one by predators. The protection comes from leaders; more than that, it comes from community. It is in a community with strong leaders that we are safe. Angels are a part of that community even though we can't see them, especially our guardian angels. They are not fairies or make-believe, nor are they people who have died, but they are real beings that are assigned to protect us and guide us.

Any farmer with goats, sheep, or other livestock will tell you that a guardian of some kind is essential. Each kind of livestock requires a different kind of defending, and different guardians defend against different predators. Each community needs different guardians to defend against different predators, and yet we live in such a culture of individualism that we believe it is all on one person to protect a family, and that one person is usually the mom. But relying on just one person leaves us isolated, alone, and doing things that we are not meant to do. We are created for community—to rely on teachers, neighbors, friends, and more—and without that, we will be taken out one by one.

And more important even than community guardians is our need for a shepherd. Without a shepherd, we will not know where to go. Jesus is our Shepherd; our priests and bishops are his stewards. It is out of love for them and for our community, both the one we live in and the Church community, that we call out our shepherds when they steer their sheep the wrong way. Just as we would if we saw a shepherd not protecting his sheep.

Fr. J told me once that the Church's teachings are meant to protect us from harm. Even the teachings that I don't understand, the ones that I thought were insane when I first thought about joining the Church. They are not a list of things not to do, but a list of safety guidelines. He gave the example of playing a basketball game on the rooftop of a tall building. Without a fence around the court, that game would be dangerous. We would have to assess every move to make sure we didn't fall off the roof. But with a fence, we can play safely and enjoy the game. That fence is the Church's teachings.

When I began to look at the teachings that way and dive into asking how these teachings keep me safe, it opened up a lot of my faith for me. I still have many questions, and I get very angry when I see the Church shutting down conversations rather than engaging with people's big questions about all the big things. But now I also see that fence of the Church's teachings as something built by a healthy community and its shepherds for the well-being and safety of the sheep. But to have a community, we need to step outside of the mindset that we have to do life all alone and that we do not owe anyone else anything. We have to acknowledge that we are dumb sheep, and we do best when we are in community with other sheep and following the guidance of our Good Shepherd.

# 3.
# PRAYER WORKS. GET LIFE INSURANCE ANYWAY.

I became Catholic at the age of thirty-three after a very dramatic conversion. God wooed me through miraculous events, and I became the most idealistic baby Catholic to ever exist. I assumed that other Catholics had all the answers to life because while they were going to CCD classes and receiving the sacraments as children, I was being sexually abused and then later sleeping around. My entire life up until that moment on that road in Rome when I was surrounded by sheep led by an ancient shepherd was a long series of mistakes, bad choices, and one-night stands.

Because I was so sure that I had absolutely no concept of how to make good choices, I just followed what I saw everyone else doing. That included praying Rosaries and novenas. It meant finding the patron saint of whatever problem I was having and trying to create this magical combo of holiness and devotion that could help me with everything from dealing with my husband's struggle with addiction to my dishwasher breaking. In case you were wondering, St. Jude works for both.

But then in March of 2017, my son Anthony died by suicide in my home while I was in the drive-through at Chick-fil-A.

For months before his suicide, I knew that Anthony was in trouble. He had been at the bedside of my Tio Roy with me when they took Tio off life support. The weeks leading up to my Tio's death were the kind of heartbreaking situation that nobody could have prepared us for. My Tio did not die a peaceful death, and Anthony took it very hard because my Tio was like a father to both of us. Anthony spent summers with Tio. They would go fishing and watch TV together. They were very close. Anthony was never the same after that funeral.

A few months after Tio's death, Anthony began having episodes of delusional thinking. I don't know what caused them, but I do know that a lot of little things occurred that brought up past traumas. I worried more and more each time something like that happened. Anthony began acting out of character, including quitting his job out of the blue. He had worked since he was sixteen, and he had two children. Healthy Anthony would never have quit working and providing for his family. I begged everyone I could think of to help me get him some help. I called my ex-husband (who Anthony considered his dad); I called Anthony's biological father and his family—but he convinced everyone that I was being dramatic. It does not help that I am, in fact, a huge drama queen. It was the first time in Anthony's twenty-two years of life that I had ever contacted his biological dad or his family for help with Anthony. That is how desperate I was.

Eventually, I began to pray novenas for him. Weeks before his suicide, the relics of St. Anthony of Padua were in Austin, and I drove into the city to venerate them. I asked God to help Anthony find his way back to him. Years earlier, Anthony had told me he was an atheist. I was upset and argued with him for months. It didn't help. He was sure of himself the way that all twenty-something-year-olds are, and now it seemed like God was the only one who could help him.

In addition to my novenas, I had priests offering up Masses for Anthony to get better, and tons of friends were praying for him. Still, on a beautiful Wednesday in March, he hanged himself in the garage of the first house I ever owned. The house he was so happy about when we told him and his siblings that it was ours. The house that he had his first room in. The house he brought his first child home to days after she was born. The house that we had celebrated holidays in. The house that he walked into on the night before his suicide asking me if he could stay the night.

I had made dinner that night, and as the police officers were in the garage covering Anthony's body and doing whatever it is that police do in that situation, I stood at the kitchen sink, finally cleaning up the dishes from the night before and staring at the piece of meatloaf Anthony had left on his plate. It seemed so incredibly stupid that he was lying dead in the garage, and his leftover meatloaf was still in the sink.

A few weeks after Anthony's funeral, I saw a story on Facebook of a kid who had almost drowned in a body of water in our old community. Somehow, his mom had caught his arm right before he went under and saved him. The comments from the people in my community sent me into a rage. Things like, "God has a plan for that young man's life!" made me want to set my phone on fire. Yeah? Does God only have a plan for some of us and the rest of us can just die?

Months after that, I saw another story of a child who was prayed for and lived. People commented, "Prayer works!" and I thought, *Sure it does.* I had prayed for my child. I had begged God to save Anthony's life and bring him back to me. I had walked up to the tabernacle and told Jesus that I needed him to do something because my kid was in a bad way and I didn't know how to help him. And yet, while I ordered a twelve-piece nugget meal at Chick-fil-A, Anthony was finding the belt that he would use to take his own life. As I walked from my car to the door of my house, I heard him kick the stool out from under himself, and I had no idea what that sound was until his body was gone and I saw the stool turned on its side on the ground. All of this had me asking the question of how exactly this is "prayer working," because it felt like the opposite of working to me.

It took me almost a year of yelling and telling God he sucked at his job before I could begin praying again. In Advent of 2017, I finally asked God to help me with my anger, because I felt my humanity slipping. I hated everyone. Especially the people posting cheerfully on Facebook. I made a deal with God that I would go to Confession and let it all out *if* my favorite priest came to my parish to hear Confessions. My parish does a Confession marathon for Advent and Lent, so I knew it was pretty probable, but I was not going to seek it out. The next morning I woke up, and the first thing on my Facebook newsfeed was the names of the priests hearing Confession. My favorite priest was the first name on the list.

I walked into the confessional and kept my promise. I confessed my anger that other people's kids were living while mine was dead. It seemed cruel and unfair. I confessed that I was furious with God for standing there watching my son die. How hard would it have been to have the belt break? Or for me to have found him after hearing the stool turn over? He is God; if he can instruct Moses through a burning bush, I did not think it was unreasonable for him to have stepped in and saved my son's life. I confessed how rude it was for people to think God did not have a plan for Anthony's life, which is how I took those exaltations of "God saved _____ because he has a plan for his life." I was angry on a level that transcended anything I had ever felt before, which is saying something.

I did not have to explain myself to this priest. He had been hearing my Confessions for seven years by that point. He heard my first Confession when I admitted to a lifetime of sleeping with any man who gave me even the smallest compliment. He heard my Confession when I said I thought

Catholics were insane and still living in the dark ages. There
was nothing that he had not heard me confess; I knew I was
safe.

That is when the reality of the Sacrament of Confession
hit me. Not only was this man my friend and my priest. Not
only had he been with me on my best day (my wedding day)
and my worst day—the day Anthony died. He acted *in per-
sona Christi* in my life. Like, literally, he was acting as Jesus in
this room where I was laying down all my anger, grief, and
envy. He was not looking at me like I was a psycho for not
being happy that other people's kids were living. He looked
at me like a man who knew the life lost in Anthony's death—
both because Father loved Anthony and also because he
knew God knew Anthony. God knew the tragedy in Anthony's suicide. The loss of Anthony's future, the devastating
fact that Anthony saw taking his life as an option or solution.

When I finally finished my Confession, I walked out of
there a hundred pounds lighter and certain that God loved
me.

I also walked out of there understanding that Anthony's
death was not how it was supposed to happen, but that we
will all meet it at some point. Maybe we don't survive a car
crash or a swim in the ocean that takes us under. Maybe we
go peacefully in our sleep or, like my Tio, after the crushing
decision to be taken off of life support. But one day each of
us will die no matter how hard we pray to live. Dying is not
a failure of our prayers or a failure of God in answering
them; it is the cost of sin. We pray and we tell him what we
want because we love God, not because he is our genie that

we boss around to grant all our wishes. Death is a part of life. We have to process some deaths more than others. I will never not miss my son. The sword in my heart is permanent, yet at the same time, people die.

We can and should pray all we want, but we also need to buy life insurance and plan our own funerals (so our children do not have to), because again, people die. It is the cost of sin. The hard things might be easier with faith, but they don't go away. We have to have conversations with our parents, children, and spouses about where we want to be buried. Because the hard things are also made a bit easier when we face them, rather than tell ourselves that God will make them all go away.

I also feel like we need to have deeper conversations about death, grief, and trauma. Not everything we think about grief is true. People are not "strong" when they aren't visibly crushed by grief. That implies that those who show their emotions are "weak," and that is just false. Everyone grieving is doing the best they can to survive. Whether that is by lying on the couch binge-watching *Hoarders* and telling God he needs new training on being God or by working harder than ever and writing award-winning books. Both are successful ways of grieving. One is not better than the other. The only wrong way to grieve is by picking up a drug habit—which I thought of, but I was too attached to my couch and too invested in *Hoarders* to chase a score.

We could also use an overhaul on how we talk about prayer. I don't know if my prayers that Anthony would find his way back to God were answered because I don't know if Anthony, as a grown man with free will, chose to accept the gift of salvation. He lived his life as an adult who knew the teaching of the Church and walked away from her. But whether my prayers were answered has nothing to do with finding the magic combo of novenas and saints. It has to do with me asking God for something, talking to him about it, and accepting whatever happens, even if it is the outcome I least want. You pray for a miracle, but you also buy life insurance.

# 4.
# GRIEF HUMOR

After Anthony's suicide, the greatest gift my pastor gave me was the permission to laugh even in the middle of my worst nightmare. My pastor and I have always shared quips and snarky back-and-forths as a sign of affection. Father is one of the funniest people I know, but his sense of humor is dry and sometimes dark, which is why we get along so well. He nicknamed me Morticia Adams, and he once came over for Halloween and he got a kick telling everyone he spent it with the Adams family.

The afternoon that we found Anthony dead in the garage, my pastor was the first person I called while my husband and third son, Gabe, got on the phone with 911. I told Father that Anthony was dead and begged him to come to the house. At the time, I didn't really know why I needed him. Now, I can tell you that at that moment, I needed a parent, a father. Father rushed to the house, and on his way he called Fr. J, who had baptized Anthony and celebrated my wedding.

When Father arrived, he looked both confused and angry. Before he could say anything, I announced, "He is having a Catholic funeral." His reply was, "Of course he is. I wouldn't fight with you on a good day; I sure as hell wouldn't fight with you now." I laughed. The sound that came out of my mouth seemed so wrong because just feet from me in the garage was my son's dead body. Then I said, "I gave up Dr Pepper for Lent, and as soon as the cops leave I am going to go get the biggest Dr Pepper I can find. God will just have to deal with it."

I did not know it then, but in making me laugh and accepting my decision to break my Lenten fast, Father gave me permission to grieve my own way for Anthony. I did not know at that time that he had also faced huge losses, including the deaths of babies he had baptized and loved ones. He ministered to me with his own authenticity that gave me the green light to grieve as I needed to. He never told me that everything would be OK. When I said "I cannot do this" about some aspect of making funeral arrangements or living without Anthony, he reminded me that I had no choice; I had to do it. I spent weeks and months after Anthony's funeral watching *Hoarders*. Something about that show helped me feel *seen*, especially as piles of stuff built up in my house and the front yard went longer and longer without being mowed. I felt like defending the hoarders on the show from people's judgments. Horrible things happen, and when they do, who the hell cares about cutting the grass or cleaning out the fridge? It's all just stupid.

Then, while lying in bed with matted hair on a Tuesday afternoon in clothes that I had been wearing for a week, I watched an episode with a woman who had lost a child in a traumatic way. When the psychologist opened her freezer, she discovered the worst part of this poor woman's hoarding: the freezer was full of dead cats. The doctor looked at the woman and asked, "What happened?" The woman said, "My son died, but I'm fine. I pick these cats up so they won't be alone." It was the "I'm fine" coming from this woman who was clearly not fine that got me to reach over to my side table and grab my phone to text "I am not fine; I need an appointment" to my therapist.

Father gave me permission to grieve in whatever way I needed. *Hoarders* gave me the jolt I needed to start living again in the midst of my grief.

With my therapist, I began processing the suicide of my oldest son and all the ways that my own trauma and pain impacted the lives of my children. That work was so sad and depressing that I coped by watching anything funny I could find on Netflix, including comedy specials and *Grace and Frankie*. I needed balance. Comedy gave me that.

One of the comedians I discovered was Felipe Esparza. I stumbled across his special on Netflix, and it made me laugh until I couldn't breathe. Like those episodes of *Hoarders*, it made me feel *seen*. Felipe has a Spanish accent like my Tios and cousins, and a lot of his jokes are things that I get as someone who grew up in a Tejano/Mexican American family. It is rare to find a comedian that really speaks to the experience of being American but also not. We have one foot on each side of the border, only some of us have never crossed the Rio Grande. It is a really strange thing that only we know, so the inside jokes are numerous. (The jokes are also not rated G, so do not go watch his specials and then send me an email telling me how scandalized you are, because I'm warning you now.) What I love about Felipe most, though, is his backstory.

Felipe was a drug addict. He was a teen dad, and then he struggled with drug addiction. One day his mother, in an act of desperation, called a priest named Fr. G and asked him to come over and try to get Felipe some help. It turned out that Felipe needed a place to go anyway because he had gotten into a fight with someone in his neighborhood who was now out to kill him. So he accepted help from Fr. G, which turned into his first step in his journey into comedy.

Felipe's story reminds me of my own. It also reminds me of what Noe Rocha said to me when I first washed up on the banks of the Catholic Church looking for something that I had lost hope in finding. Noe said, "God loves you more than you think he does." And that is so true. It is as true for me as it is for a comedian from LA or for the lady who is so deep in mourning that she picks up dead cats and takes them home so they won't be alone. God helps us all, and he waits for us to show up so that he can take care of us. That does not mean he removes all suffering from our lives—in fact, I have suffered more and more the longer I am in a personal relationship with him—but he does not abandon us.

There is humor in all things, and that is what comedy reminds me of. In the midst of the worst moments in my

life, I could find something to laugh at. And so could my
children.

Anthony had five brothers and a best friend who was like
his brother. This is the perfect number of brothers to have
when you die by suicide and find yourself needing pallbearers. Go figure. Maybe he thought of that and knew that at
least that would be one less thing for me to worry about,
or maybe it was just happenstance—either way, he had his
pallbearers, so that was marked off my list of things to deal
with. That is, until his biological father and his half-brother
decided they would like to help carry Anthony's casket as
the one act of support they ever showed him. I figured it
was better late than never, so I allowed it. My boys were not
happy about it and neither was my ex-husband, who is and
will always be Anthony's dad. But nobody fought me on
anything because, like my pastor said, fighting me on a good
day doesn't usually turn out well, so nobody was willing to
test me on the day of my son's funeral. Everyone was just
counting their blessings that I had, up to this point, not lost
it altogether.

Anthony was a gym rat. He loved working out. He was
tiny his entire life until he began lifting weights. So at his
funeral on either side of the casket there were my two sons
in the front, my three stepsons and Anthony's best friend,
Caleb, behind them, and Anthony's biological father and
his son in the back. Gabe has always been the funny one of
all my children. Anthony would pitch him jokes, and Gabe
would land them. It was their thing. So there's Gabe with my
second oldest, Dan, across from him in this stupid situation

where they are carrying a box with their dead brother in it and the bio dad and brother Anthony hardly knew were in the back helping. What does Gabe do? Crack a joke, of course. When the funeral director said, "OK, pick up the casket, place it in the hearse, and roll it forward," Gabe saw an opening. He looked at Dan and then back at his stepbrothers, Caleb, and the two in the back, and asked, "Are y'all ready to deadlift this bad boy?!" Everyone there who knew Anthony and his love for Gabe's sense of humor began to laugh. Gabe smiled from ear to ear because in that moment he was everything Anthony had taught him to be: funny and in the spotlight. He honored Anthony with that joke.

Anthony was the life of our family. His jokes were classic, and he loved to play pranks on me and his siblings. Once he buried Gabe in the backyard, and he annoyed Dan, who hates pranks, to the max with his antics. Anthony created most of our family's inside jokes. His sense of humor was unmatched except for Gabe's, and Gabe has lost a little bit of that spark he always had in the aftermath of losing his big brother.

One of our family songs is "I'm N Luv (Wit a Stripper)," by T-Pain. It is the perfect song other than the lyrics; our family loves the beat and the rhythm of the lyrics, and the flow is amazing. As we followed the hearse with Anthony and our priest in it, we listened to all of our family songs, including that one. I specifically rented a car with a sound system that would bump it hard because that is what Anthony would have liked. But in doing that I forgot that everyone behind us were good Catholics and that Fr. J was in front of us with Anthony. So everyone heard us blasting "I'm N Luv (Wit a Stripper)" as we sobbed. That is one of my cherished memories that I know will go through my head on the day I die as I look back at my life. Because it is beautiful and also hilarious. Is this how every family would grieve? No. We have got to be the only family who would mourn the loss of our Anthony by listening to that song. But it's how we were able to get through the gate into the cemetery, and I still laugh-cry when I hear it.

What all of this—watching comedy specials and *Hoarders*, laughing at jokes and bumping music in a funeral procession—has shown me is that even in the worst of times, God is with me. He mourns with me, he laughs with me, he shakes his head at me, and he honors my unique sense of humor and does not expect me to be anyone else. He delights in me every moment of my life, even the moments when I am laugh-crying at how good a song "I'm N Luv (Wit a Stripper)" is. God is with me always. In the good times and in the most horrible times. And at moments when I am at my lowest, he throws me an inside joke, like a post on Facebook about a plant that looks like a penis that traps flies, just to see me smile. God is the funniest person I know. He loves me enough to make me laugh.

# 5.
# YOUR KIDS NEED YOU TO HEAL, NOT DIE FOR THEM

I became a mother at the age of sixteen when I got knocked up by a neighbor. As much as I loved my oldest son, the entire story of how he came to exist was rooted in my childhood trauma. And my childhood trauma was rooted in my mother's trauma, which was rooted in her mother's trauma, and on and on. All of it can be traced back to colonialism and white supremacy. I know that line might make some of you want to close this book and dismiss me as "woke." But I ask you this, if the past sins of people we have never met and who seem to have nothing to do with us do not have an impact on current situations, then what is Baptism for?

The truth is that Catholics do believe that the sins of the past, of people we have never met and whose actions we had no part in, affect us. That is why we have the sacraments, and it is specifically what the Sacrament of Baptism is all about.

The reality is that the entire story of human history is about sin and God finding ways to heal us from it. In the beginning, Adam and Eve listened to the snake in the garden and let their mistrust of God's love, sowed in them by the snake, cause them to disobey him. Ever since that moment, God has been reconciling us to himself through healing. Healing is about us going back to how it was in "the beginning," as in Genesis.

The Genesis account inspired Pope John Paul II to create his theology of the body. Maybe we've focused on the sexuality and marriage parts of that teaching while failing to look at the whole picture of how God creates us, what sin does to that, and how Jesus became human to die for us and heal us so we could be reconciled with God. All of it began with people we do not know doing something we are not responsible for that has an effect on us today. God became human to heal every one of us. Every system is made up of broken human beings, and every human being is made up of systems. That is what is mind-blowing about the theology of the body; it is not just about certain parts of the body, or just the reproductive system—it is about the whole person. Sex is a part of who we are, but it is not all there is to us. More than that, we are relational. Another word for that is communal.

Every system in our body is created to function as part of the whole. This is how God made us. The part that interests me the most is how our brain works with our entire body to handle trauma. Our fight, flight, or freeze response is rooted in survival. We are now living in an age where basic survival is not an issue for many of us, and we can begin to understand trauma. This includes its impact on our lives, the lives of those that came before us, and the lives of those that will come after us. More than that, we can begin to understand how trauma affects our relationships and how our healing from trauma can in turn heal those relationships, which can help us build healthy communities in our families and beyond.

Here's the thing—we carry trauma in our DNA. We also get traumatized through the experiences of life, putting trauma on top of trauma. The fact that we live in a culture that discourages rest and self-care and that tries to give us quick, easy steps to find happiness only makes it harder for us to heal from our trauma.

Healing was the main mission of Jesus. He healed people's bodies, but his primary aim was healing them spiritually. Everything he did was about healing, including dying on the Cross for us and rising from the dead. In fact, rising from the dead is the ultimate healing. Healing from our trauma is how we live our best life and our best eternity. And yet, we so often fight it because it sucks. It is a long process that costs us everything. To me, healing feels like being nailed to a cross. Who volunteers for that? Nobody. We have to find ourselves with no other choice. Jesus wasn't exactly the most cheerful about his Cross either. He prayed for the cup to pass him, but when there was no other option, he went to be beaten and tortured and hung on a cross. I often forget that he said to follow him meant the same fate. I felt that when going through therapy.

Nothing was harder for me than going to therapy and facing all the mistakes that I made as a mother. I can easily look back at my life and point out all the things I did wrong; it is much harder not to gloss over the impact all those mistakes had on my children. It has been even harder to look at them in the aftermath of Anthony's suicide. So I get why people avoid doing it. It is so much easier to read a book on the five ways to manifest your best life than to sit with a therapist and examine all the times you screwed up as a parent. It is easier to look at your star chart or a personality test and blame your failures as a parent on those things than it is to face how the fear of abandonment instilled in you as a kid makes you go from people pleasing to burning everything down in five minutes flat, depending on the situation (*cough cough*, looking at myself here).

I used to say things like "if anyone hurts my kids, I will kill them" or "I would walk through fire to keep my kids safe," but the reality is that I did not do either of those things. And even worse, it was me and my bad choices that hurt them, and I refused to walk through fire and face my mistakes until I was thirty-three. In some ways, I was too late. I regret not going sooner. I am not responsible for my son's suicide, but I can't help but wonder how things would be different if I had faced my mistakes sooner.

So what is healing?

Like all things Catholic, we have to start from the beginning. In the beginning God made Adam and Eve, the sun, moon, stars, and all the animals, and it was good. We know the story. Everyone was happy, and God came to visit his creatures in the cool of the evening. That is where we are all supposed to be, in the Garden of Eden communing with God. But then the snake came along and convinced us that there is more to life. We believed that stupid snake, and *bam*, we hurt ourselves and others. Adam hurt Adam, and he also hurt Eve. Eve hurt Eve, and in the process also hurt Adam. Their relationship was wounded, and so was their relationship with God. They became scared of him, and they passed those fears and wounds to their kids, who passed them to us. The root of all the bad things—colonialism, racism, sexism, and all the other bad isms—is that moment in the garden when Adam and Eve decided that God did not want the best for them and took things into their own hands. All the pain in the world is rooted in that one moment.

Jesus came into the world to heal it. But he is not magic. He does not wave a wand and everyone is healed and everything is fine. If only it was that easy. None of this is easy, and that is the cost of love. God loves us enough to give us free will to choose to respond to his love. He knew that we would abuse that free will over and over, making things more difficult than he planned them to be, but he gave it to us anyway because God wants us to choose to love him back. There is no magic fast track to healing. Not going to Lourdes, not going to healing Masses, not going to Confession. All of those things are ways to receive healing, but they still come with the need for repentance and a change in direction.

The word for this change in direction is *metanoia*. I learned this word when I was in RCIA with Noe Rocha. Noe is a walking saint. Not because he is perfect and has made no mistakes or even is not making them right now, but because he loves Jesus. Not in a televangelist kind of way, but with the kind of love that is written all over his face and that shows in the little things in life. Metanoia is not just any change in direction, but a radical 180-degree turn in the opposite direction. That change is not easy because it begins with the acknowledgment that you are going the wrong way. It also is not easy because it is not done once in life and then everything is fine. Life has a lot of 180-degree turns. Healing, repentance, and conversion happen over and over in life. Just when I think that I'm going in the right direction, I learn something about myself and have to repent all over again.

As for me, I was born into trauma and made out of trauma and then got my own trauma. Everything I did from age thirteen until thirty-three was some form of reaction to all of that trauma. My need to be liked, and also my habit of lighting everything on fire when I felt the slightest threat of not being liked. The way I treated myself and others. The fact that I slept with anyone who paid me the slightest compliment. All of it.

When I was sixteen, my cousin got married to a girl who lived next door to me. That girl had an older brother. He was handsome at the wedding with a cowboy hat, Wranglers, and boots. That picture in my head of him asking me to dance with a smile that made me melt is what keeps me from hating his guts for everything that happened in the next twenty-three years. That same smile painted the most handsome face I have ever seen, the face of our son, Anthony. I would be lying, though, if I said that the only thing that attracted me to the man was his smile. It was also that he asked me to dance and not my cousin Dana, who was practically peeing on herself trying to get his attention. That sense of being better than her is what motivated me to say yes to that dance, which months later led to Anthony being conceived in the back of a car. I have spent twenty-seven years telling myself that I really liked my son's biological father, but the God's honest truth is that I liked not being the loser in my family for once. I got the boy, and my cousin did not. That kind of pettiness and spite has been the fire behind so many of the choices I have made in life.

I never really understood that, though. I was just blowing through life. I did not examine why I did things or consider the consequences. I just did it.

Through a decade in therapy I learned a lot about myself and about the pain I had been living in. I was born without a father to a mother who did not know how to be warm and kind. I was raped and molested from the age of five until I was nine, when I started my period and my abuser finally left me alone because he didn't want to get me pregnant. I have had my period since I was nine, a suffering that I think needs acknowledgment because *holy moly* do periods suck. My entire life I have been a fatherless child who feels abandoned and unloved. I have made desperate choices to try and squeeze any drops of care out of anyone I can. I have abandoned my children to do it. That is the root of my pain now. I cannot go back. I cannot change any of it. I can just try to be better.

So when I tell parents of small children to do the hard thing and go to therapy, it is because they still have a chance that I will never have: to start the healing process when their kids are young so that they can be the best parents they can be. This advice works for people without kids too, because the best thing we can do for ourselves and all of our relationships is to heal.

The part about relationships that we do not talk about enough is how they require us to show up as our real self, not the self that is hidden behind the wounds, the trauma reactions, the defense mechanisms. The only way that you can show up in a relationship as your real self is to process your trauma and wounds and to allow God to heal them. That is what your kids need from you. Your trauma is the fire you have to walk through for them.

With every healing moment we become more and more of the person God made us to be. We still bear scars of the wounds, but they are no longer bleeding on us and everyone around us. We get to be who we are now and not who we used to be—even though, in so many ways, who we are now is the same person, but how we act is totally different.

Everything Jesus did was to heal us. He knew that we carry a lot of baggage. Some of it is ours, some is our ancestors'. He came to lift it all from our shoulders. But we have to acknowledge that it's there. We have to look at ourselves, face our faults and bad choices, and repair the damage they caused. Not only do we have to do this as individuals, but we also have to do it as communities and as a Church. That is how we get back to the beginning, when Adam and Eve communed directly with God. The beginning is the entire point; it is what we were made for.

## 6.
# HOW TO TRAIN YOUR DRAGON

Anger has always been an immediate reaction for me. Ever since I was a little kid, anger was my emotional response to anything that I felt was unjust or scary. When my mother spanked me, I would cry hot tears and lash out in anger, telling her that she was a horrible mother and that one day I would leave and never return. I was only five. I kept that promise too. As soon as I could, I began running away. I was a chronic runaway from the age of thirteen until I got pregnant with my first child. Each time I ran away, what fueled me to move past my fear of the unknown was my anger.

When Anthony died, I decided that I could no longer believe in God because he had stood by and watched my son die. Two days after my son's suicide, I got dressed and went to 6 a.m. Mass at my parish. After Mass was over, my husband kneeled against the pew with his head bowed, and he began sobbing. Person after person came by and comforted him. I sat right next to him, dry-eyed, and people just looked past me. I was so angry that I got up, pushed past my husband, and headed straight to the tabernacle to tell God exactly how I felt about everything. I cussed him up and down in my head.

Later on, a woman told me that she had seen me that morning and thought about how strong my faith was to go to God like that after my son's suicide. I laughed out loud at that, because there was nothing holy or faithful about the way I was talking to God in that moment. I told him that I was leaving that church and never speaking to him again. I had tried life his way and it was a huge nope now for me because he did *nothing* to save my child's life. And then I told him how much I hated everyone feeling sorry for my husband and looking past me, Anthony's mother, as if I did not matter. As if, because I was not sobbing in my seat, I was not totally destroyed. I told the woman all this, and she just looked at me blankly. The poor woman thought she had witnessed a saintlike response to a parent's child dying by suicide, and now she knew the truth: what she had really witnessed was a woman breaking up with God.

I was so angry, but even in that anger, I kept talking to God. Well, I didn't "talk"; I ranted. Either way, I was still in some form of communication with him. I knew where to find him: at Mass. So that is why I kept going. Eventually, my ranting to God made me find my way back to the Sacrament of Confession, which has always been where God and I are the most honest with each other.

My husband and I once went to Confession to an elderly Irish priest. Stacey went first. I don't know what he confessed, but he told me when he came out that the priest bopped him on the head with his cane after he finished. So I was a little scared as I walked into the confessional. When I was done confessing all of my sins, all of them rooted in anger, the priest looked at me and, in his thick Irish accent, said, "Anger is how you survived horrible things, but it does not serve you anymore." You might think that would be the last time I confessed sins rooted in anger. You would be wrong. I have been to so many Confessions where I laid out things I said or thought or did in anger. Horrible things. Wishing bad things on others. I had a great Nigerian priest tell me that my anger was like a wild dog, and I needed to chain it to a tree.

It was not until I watched the final few episodes of *Game of Thrones* that God got through to me about the dangers of my anger. Let me just say that if you don't want the show spoiled for you, then now is the time to skip ahead a few pages. And if you are tempted to stop reading because you heard that *Game of Thrones* is of the devil, please give me a chance; you do not have to watch it to get my point.

In the last few episodes of the show, the justice warrior Daenerys has found her match in the villain Queen Cersei. Dany has worked hard to conquer oppressors and set enslaved people free. She has fought for women and for soldiers denied their humanity for the sake of those they defend. Her entire quest has been to free captives and bring about a just world by claiming her rightful place on the throne. But little by little, her fight for justice brought her to do things that were questionable. By the time she came head to head with Cersei, queen of oppressors, Dany had made concessions in morality in the name of justice. So when Cersei beheads Dany's best friend in front of her, Dany loses it. She jumps on her dragon, and in her grief and anger, she commands the beast to burn the entire city down to ash. Women, children, animals, and anything else in the path of Dany and her dragon were burned to nothing.

As I watched the scene unfold on TV, I could sense God staring at me. You know that stare you get when you are watching or hearing something that the person staring at you thinks you really need to take in because it applies to you? The stare you act like you do not feel on the side of your whole head? That stare. I knew God was waiting for me to admit that I got it. And he knew I got it because he is God, but he always waits to hear me acknowledge that I see what he wants me to see before we get into the discussion. That is the thing about God; he does not speak at us, he waits as long as he has to for us to step into the conversation freely and be ready to talk and listen. I once heard motivational speaker and spiritual teacher Iyanla Vanzant say that when you tell someone something they are not ready to hear, it is like throwing a dodgeball at them, knowing they can't catch it and that they will get hit in the face. It is an act of violence, she said. God is not violent. He waits until we are ready to hear and talk to him about what he is trying to tell us.

I watched the show thinking that the face on this character looked familiar. The whole thing did. Dany's anger looked sad, hurt, and irrational. I had seen that face so many times staring back at me from a reflection in a window, a rearview mirror, or in the shades of someone's sunglasses. It was the face of pain and fear masked as anger.

For the next few days after watching that episode I thought of those two priests, the Irish priest who told me that anger had helped me survive and the Nigerian priest who told me to chain it up to a tree. I thought about how anger was my own dragon, ready to turn anyone who hurt me into ash and sometimes even those who did nothing to me but somehow ended up guilty in my mind for being a part of my pain. I thought of how much I loved my dragon, my anger. How safe it made me feel and how close we had become as it kept me safe so I could survive. How chaining it to a tree and walking away when it had helped me live through horrible things would be hard. It is a loss. So much so that sometimes I still let it off its chain.

I have a pit bull named Bourbon. He is my dog, and I love him so much. He has also bitten people. The second time he bit someone I was sure he was going to be put down, and I was crying just thinking about it. But animal control came and told me that if I could get a certified dog trainer to work with him, they would give him another chance. So I did just that. I had to put a pinch collar on him and tell him no for the first time in his life. He learned commands, was corrected when he needed it, and he finally walked on a leash. When we moved out here to the land in an RV, there was no room for him to sleep with us, so he was told no when he jumped on the bed. Because of his training, he listened and has not tried to get on the bed. He also does not get on the couch. That is the power of training.

I think of my anger as my dragon and my anger management as dragon training. I will never be rid of anger. For one thing, it is a human emotion. For another, it has been my way to cope since I was a tiny child. So instead of pretending that I can ever rid myself of it, I train it. When I get angry, I acknowledge that I am in fact angry. Then I ask myself a lot of questions. Am I angry about something the other person did, or am I triggered about something else? Am I tired, hungry, or sleepy? Should I express my feelings, or do I need to wait until I calm down? When I do unleash on someone and hurt them, I make reparations, in a way that they know about. This does not mean that people get to walk all over me. Sometimes I express my anger justly. For that, I make no apologies. I have the right to stand up for myself and others. But I cannot use standing up for myself as an excuse for being a jerk. If I am confused about which one it is, I ask God. He has no problem letting me know.

# 7.
# OUR LADY OF HOT MESSES

I don't think we give Mary enough credit for all the hard things she survived. We have this idea that her life was easy even though we can pick up our Bibles any time and read for ourselves that it was not. She had an angel come to her when she was fifteen and tell her she was going to be the Mother of God. I don't know if you remember being fifteen, but that for sure was a seriously intense moment. I got pregnant at sixteen, so trust me, I know that being a teen mother is not without chaos.

Then there was the whole no-room-at-the-inn situation. Riding a donkey while nine months pregnant? No fun. I am sure Joseph got on her nerves. Then, after she has this baby in a barn, suddenly they are back on the run because some jackwagon is killing all babies under the age of two to make sure that he does not lose his power and privilege. You get the point. Mary, like all of us, survived some crazy stuff. And grief. She lost her husband and her Son. Mary had a hard life. You would think that someone who carried God in her womb would have it easy, but that was clearly not the case.

Now, was Mary a hot mess? I don't think so. What I do know is that during my entire life, the one person who I felt got me and my issues was Mary. I used to think that she was judging me because she was sinless, but after Anthony's suicide, I began to see that she is just a mother. Just a woman. Just a human being. She does not think or even consider that she is better than me or anyone else. She loves us. She is our mother as well. Which means she cares for us deeply as we are, even when we are drunk in a bar at 2:15 p.m. when we are supposed to be picking up our kids from school. Does she know we are wrong? Yes. But does she stop loving us and praying for us to stop forgetting our kids after school? No, she 100 percent does not.

Mary and I have had a long relationship. My mother used to light candles to her in prayer for me to stop being crazy. I was a very traumatized teenager who was living in reaction to that trauma. I got a lot of my trauma reaction genes from my grandmother. Both of us tried to use anger to heal from our pain. This meant that I was very mean to my mother. I yelled, hit, kicked, stole keys, slammed doors, destroyed TVs, and pulled phones out of walls. There were reasons for my anger, mainly my being raped and molested for years, with my abuser living in the same house until I was fifteen. At thirteen, after I chickened out on having sex with my first boyfriend and he broke up with me to sleep with my best friend, I decided that I needed to have sex with boys so that would not happen again. What I learned from this experience and from everything that had happened to me as a child was that sex is how you get men to love you and never leave you. So I began to sneak out of my window to see a man in his twenties; then I started running away. I wanted out of my house, away from my mom and away from the man who had abused me. I did not know how to say that. First, all I knew how to do was let my anger boil over. Later, all I knew how to do was run.

I have been running all my life, it seems. I would leave before someone left me. I would get someone before they got me. I wouldn't let people close to me because I thought that if they knew me, they would leave, and then I had to leave before they left me. I lived in this paranoid cycle of self-loathing until I met Ben, my first husband. We had our own dysfunctional relationship, but he was the first man that I knew with all of my heart loved me. I have never doubted that. But he had his own traumas that made him unable to love me fully. We were two traumatized young adults trying our best to help each other heal without a clue on how to do that.

A few months after our wedding, I was pregnant. We were so happy. We were married, he was working, and we had just bought a new truck. Our apartment was in a cute little complex with a garden and pool. Anthony was almost four, and he and I walked the complex and swam in the pool while Ben worked. For me, the baby was the sign of a new, stable life with my family. Unlike the last time I was pregnant, now I was married, my husband loved me, and we were a family.

At the twenty-week sonogram I looked at the black-and-gray video and saw my baby's head, feet, and hands. I could see the eyes and nose clearly. It was exciting to see this little human being who was going to finally make me a legit wife and mother, not a teenager who got knocked up. But then the tech looked at me and said she had to get the doctor. The air in the room changed. The doctor came in, did his own examination, put the sonogram wand down, and then looked me in the eye and said, "Your baby does not have a heartbeat."

Those words changed everything. We lost the baby. The D&C was not for three days, which meant I walked around carrying my dead child for seventy-two hours. I ate Tylenol PM and chain-smoked Newports the entire time. After the surgery nobody told me if the baby was a girl or a boy. Nobody offered grief counseling or asked us if we wanted a burial. Our family said stupid things like "It wasn't God's timing for you to have a baby," as if this child did not already exist and die. Ben tried to comfort me by taking me to dinner at Olive Garden. I sobbed into my lasagna.

After that loss, our marriage went downhill. Ben began using drugs again, which is how I learned that he had already been using before we met, and we fought all the time. I left; he followed; we made up, and the entire cycle would begin again. Eventually, I got pregnant again, but when Daniel was born, he was in and out of the hospital for the first two years of his life, first with jaundice and then twice with respiratory syncytial virus. I also went to jail for tickets when he was four weeks old. I was breastfeeding him and had to go sit in a jail for driving to work without a license or car insurance. My son was put on formula so he could eat, and I went to my six-week checkup in handcuffs. Daniel is now on three medications for anxiety and depression, which, from everything I have learned about the neuroscience of trauma, I know is rooted at least in part in his hospital stays and my arrest. All of it was a mess. And that is just the tip of the iceberg of the hot mess my life has been and how that mess has impacted the lives of my children.

At some point when I began publicly speaking about my life and my conversion to Catholicism I began to describe myself as a "hot mess," and then everyone in the curated content world of social media began to use that term as well. It was a label that made me feel less worthless and like maybe none of this was my fault. It is true that there are so many things that were not in my control. I was not in control of being sexually abused; I was not in control of being born to a Brown family with a Native American background marked by the trauma of colonization. I was not in control of the systems put in place to force me to conform in order to survive. But I was in control of my choices. One of those choices became clear to me one day in therapy: I had the choice to stay a hot mess or to start changing and cleaning my life up.

Not everyone has the domestic skills to have a clean house and freshly baked cookies ready when their kids walk in the door after school or the gifts to homeschool them. Man, I wish I had those gifts, honestly. But I have others. I can stand in a bathroom with a mother who lost her child to

suicide as she tells me all the painful, gory details of the day
she lost her child. It's a story not many people can handle
hearing but that she had to handle living through. I can tell
a story like nobody's business. I can make people laugh even
when I'm talking about the worst things that have happened
in my life. But to get to those gifts, I had to stop calling
myself a hot mess. I had to move beyond that label that
excused me from taking personal responsibility for myself
and my choices. I also had to make the decision to see my
mother as a human being who did the very best she could to
raise me and give me everything I needed, including helping
me raise my children. I owe her gratitude that I have failed
to show her for most of my life.

Our power comes from the power to choose. Look at
Adam and Eve; they had the power to set the whole world
on fire by choosing to do the one thing God told them not
to do. We have the same power in our own choices. Am I
going to choose to sit down and type out the words to write
this book, or am I going to watch Netflix? And if the choice
is Netflix, then I have to accept that as my choice and not
beat myself up over it when my book is not done; instead,
I own that I made the choice and then do what I have to in
order to finish my book. That's it.

The same goes for all the mistakes that I made as a
daughter, mother, wife, and friend while living in trauma
reaction. I cannot change any of the choices I made, but
I can acknowledge that those choices harmed others and
accept responsibility for that harm while giving myself the
grace that I did not know better. Now that I do know better,

I am intentionally making different choices. I still make mistakes, but I'm trying not to live as a hot mess even when things around me are messy.

Our choices are our power, not our messes. Yes, Our Lady stands with us in the mess, but the whole time she is praying for us to start making choices that lead to cleaning them up.

# 8.
# GIVE EVERYTHING TO GOD, BUT GET YOUR LIFE TOGETHER

This book started with one Instagram caption where I talked about how I had to get a planner to get my life together, and someone replied that I needed to just trust God more. I do trust God. A lot. But I am also me. I have trauma brain. There is research that talks about the impact chronic, unpredictable stress and trauma have on the brain.[1] And let me tell you, the more trauma I deal with, the less I can remember things, and so a planner saves my life.

I have heard "trust God" so many times since I became Catholic. As if trusting God means not doing anything. But the Bible says that "faith by itself, if it has no works, is dead" (Jas 2:17). *Works*, people. Action is required from us. Trusting God is a series of actions, not just sitting back and letting things fall into place. Sitting back and letting things fall into place is actually called "manifestation," not trusting in God. My feelings on manifestation are complicated because I love Oprah and she advocates for manifestation, and to be really honest, I find it easier to disagree with God than with Oprah. I am only human.

Jesus is God, and he took actions to save us. He did not just chill in heaven and trust that things would work out for us. Nope, he came down to earth as a fetus in the womb of Mary, he was born in a freakin' manger, and he lived among us all. He ate, pooped, slept, and learned, and then when he was ready, he began his ministry. All of those things were action packed. He also said that if we wanted to be his disciples, we had to *take up our cross* and follow him (see Matthew 16:24). Both of those things are actions.

So for me, getting my act together was part of me trusting God. And I still do not have it together at all. But here's the thing: no matter what we have to put on the planner, we can plan our life with intention. The inability to do that in the middle of a crisis like COVID-19 has been shown to be a very bad thing. We have to learn how to discern, how to carve out time for things that are important to us, and most of all, how to make sure that God has time in each of our days because when everything falls apart, we cannot count on social media to help us. We need God.

The first thing I do in my new planner is put in my prayer time, my Mass time for the month (I like to change it up), and important feast days. Then I put in work and family time so I know that when I say yes to something, I am not going to mix up my priorities. I did this for 2019 regularly, and it was one of the best years I have ever had. I did not keep this up in 2020 or 2021, and welp, my life is crazy. I juggled a lot of things and didn't do that very well. So in November of 2021, I went and ordered my 2022 planner.

We can trust God, and we can trust that he will do amazing things for us. But he still expects us to take control of the things in our life that are ours to be responsible for. Jesus is not going to go to work for us or rain down money so that we can pay the electric bill. And the electric company is not going to accept "I am trusting God on this one" when the bill is due. Jesus isn't going to make our grocery list or pick up the groceries. We have to plan our life: Who will pick up the groceries, and when? Who is in charge of doing laundry? Who is earning money to pay the electric bill, and when are we making that payment? We cannot simply trust God to live our life. He gave it to us.

Now, planning how to live our life is not the same as grinding. It is not about maximizing our time so that we can hustle and make money. The end goal is to know what is ours to take care of and what is God's. It is about being in relationship with him rather than treating him like a vending machine of answered prayers.

I think of it like to-do lists. I discern what goes on my to-do list, what goes on my husband's, and then what goes on God's. Some things, like Anthony's salvation, are just too big for me; they're not on my list, but they are on God's. But what is on my list is praying for my son and offering up Masses for him.

The priority on my to-do list, and the first thing that ought to go in my planner, is my time spent in prayer, because not having anything more important than God is the first commandment (see Deuteronomy 5:6–7). The fact that it is the first commandment and that Jesus said the greatest commandment is to love God with all our heart, mind, and soul (see Matthew 22:37–38) means that giving God time each day and going to Mass and Confession is where all the other things I do flow from. Without the Eucharist, I am just doing my own thing rather than what I am called to do. Every gift I have has been given to me by God and should be used to serve him. Even my big mouth. Even my stubbornness. My sense of justice. My anger too. All of it and more has been given to me by God to serve him, and if I do not stay connected to the source and summit of my faith, Jesus, then I go off the rails. I use these gifts for other things. It happens all the time.

And this is why making plans helps. Knowing that I have set this time aside for Mass or for prayer means that I know when I am choosing to spend that time otherwise. And I have to own that choice if I regret it later.

Setting aside this time also helps keep me focused on my priorities. Noe Rocha once told me that our priorities have to be in the right order for our lives to be balanced. For me, those priorities are God, family, self-care, writing (which is the gift God gave me), work, and then everything else. My anxiety and impostor syndrome often manifest as perfectionism for me. It is not that I want things to be perfect, but I have convinced myself that I will fail so why even try.

Keeping focus on my priorities helps me to move past that attitude and accept myself and my flaws while also working to be better.

I also have time-management issues. I do not have that gift that some people have where they can stay up until 4 a.m. to write and then get up at 8 a.m. and go to work. It was not until writing this book that I realized I am only good at writing in the morning hours. Afternoon is a little iffy but by evening, I'm toast. I can't do it. And I've come to understand that that changes in the summer months. I did not know that you could flow with the seasons in the way you work rather than just label yourself and live like that forever.

I've also come to see that my brain functions in a certain kind of way. A planner may work for me, but that does not mean everyone will be able to use it because our brains might work differently. Wild. We are not all the same. We do not work the same way, we are not productive at the same hours, and we react differently to different seasons. We get to work with those things rather than against them. The coolest part is that we get to do that and also be in relationship with God at the same time. I know; I'm blowing your mind right now.

What does all of this have to do with planners? Well, when I go back and look through my old planners, I can see exactly what I have accomplished and when. I can see all the errands I have run and all the groceries I picked up. I can see what my days are full of and that I'm not lazy. Maybe I did watch Netflix for five hours one day, but then there were thirty other days when I did all the things I needed to do.

That day of Netflix was rest, not laziness. Once I see all the things that I have accomplished, then I can see that I am not an impostor. I am capable. I am doing things God calls me to do, and I am succeeding. In the day-to-day, it can feel like I am not accomplishing anything, but old planners give me the big picture, both the big picture behind me and the big picture in front of me.

So yes, trust God. Trust him with everything. Trust him with your everyday life, your wants, your dreams, and your needs. Trust him to show up, and have no fear that he will not love you. God loves you more than you think he does. There is nothing God would not do for you, but also, get your act together. Learn how to budget your money, plan your meals, and figure out your laundry. But most important, use the gifts that God has given you to do what he is calling you to do. If you do not know what those gifts are, then begin by pulling out your planner and setting a time for daily prayer and meditation. Go from there. Use that prayer and meditation time to ask God to show you your gifts. If you don't know how you will find the time for prayer, just look at when you are in the habit of doomscrolling, and use that block of time!

## 9.
## DOOMSCROLLING AND OTHER WAYS WE NUMB OURSELVES

When I was a kid, the bad habit we all had was standing in front of the fridge with the door open looking for something that would satisfy the emptiness we felt that was somewhere other than our stomachs. Now we try to satisfy that emptiness by scrolling on our phones, otherwise known as doomscrolling. And why is it doomy? Because there is nothing satisfying about it at all, and with every thumb swipe, we feel more and more empty.

I can tell when I have been on social media too much by how much anxiety I have. There is study after study connecting anxiety to time spent on social media. There are also a lot of articles and books about how social media algorithms feed us negative content to keep us engaged. It is not a fluke but a design choice that makes those articles about the worst things ever pop up in our feed rather than the pictures of our cousins' babies. Social media is designed to make us mad and upset because that is how we are most likely to engage with content. We get mad and then share it with our hot take and then someone comments with their opposing view and on and on. We do not engage with content that makes us happy in that way.

We have all said that everything feels like a dumpster fire these days. But the big problem is that we tend to think that the dumpster fire is over there and that those people are the problem; rarely do we see the matches we are holding and how we are part of the problem. We do not see how our own doomscrolling leaves us frustrated and angry and how our own sharing of things that others can doomscroll can contribute to them being frustrated and angry too. At some point we have to admit to ourselves that there is nothing in the fridge and nothing in our social media feeds that will fill the emptiness inside of us.

It is not just social media. As human beings, we use all kinds of things to try to fill those empty places within us. We can do it with anything: food, shopping, working out, Netflix, Hulu, sports. These things aren't bad in themselves, but they are great distractions from having to look in the mirror and work through our flaws and wounds. Sometimes they are fun distractions, or even better, they numb the pain or anxiety that is rooted in something we would rather pretend is not real. So we keep scrolling, looking for something that will motivate us to change, will give us an excuse to not change, or better yet, tell us that we are the best exactly how we are and we are so totally right about everything we think.

It is also how the devil convinces us that everything is hopeless.

After my son's suicide, I remember scrolling through Snapchat and watching my friends having a good time during spring break. I was watching people have fun on vacation, and yet for me, it was doomscrolling because every happy moment for someone else reminded me that my son was dead and I was miserable. The more I scrolled, the angrier I got and the more I lost hope.

The greatest weapon against the devil is hope. Jesus *is* Hope incarnate. And when we live through horrible things and hold onto the hope that somehow, some way, God will make things right, we resist the devil's lie that God does not love us or want what is best for us. Sometimes social media can be the voice of the serpent in the garden asking, "Does he really love you?" We have to log out and live in the life that is ours to answer, "yes, he does," because we will never see that in scrolling through the stories shared by computers that want you to be mad so that you click on more articles that make you mad.

In *Laudato si'*, Pope Francis talks about the importance of being careful about what we consume. He was talking mostly about material goods, but what really made my ears perk up was when he referred to the media we consume: the books we read and the shows we watch. I thought about social media, which is probably the media we consume the most each day.

God made us to be influenced greatly by what we consume; that is why we have the Eucharist. He gives us his
Body, Blood, soul, and divinity in the form of a piece of
bread so that we can become what we eat. Since the Eucharist shows, in a positive way, how we can be affected by what
we consume, it only makes sense that, if we are doomscrolling and consuming media that makes us feel like we are not
living our best life, we will become jealous and bitter about
the world we live in. We will become dissatisfied with our
house, our car, our children, our lack of children, our lack
of a spouse, or our spouse's breathing. If we are consuming
jealousy, anger, bitterness, and toxic positivity that tells us to
avoid our feelings and just "fake it till you make it," then we
will walk around being those things to the people who are
closest to us: our spouse, our kids, our friends, our neighbors,
and our coworkers. We become what we consume.

Social media isn't just making us discontent with our
lives. It's also giving us trauma. We can be innocently scrolling and suddenly we are watching a video of a man being
murdered or of babies who have died as their parents try
to migrate to safety. Even when we aren't stumbling across
horrible videos, we are scrolling through headlines telling
us that our country is falling apart, complaining about the
cost of gas, warning us that the environment is trashed, and
informing us of a young girl who was killed by her boyfriend
and now his skeleton has been found in the desert. All of this
bad news is too much for our brain. It is traumatic, and our
systems are not created to handle it.

Getting off social media as much as possible is a form of self-care, and I say that as someone who has checked Facebook and Instagram as I write this chapter. But when I am off social media and in my life, I am so much happier. It is so much easier to hear God and to listen to what he is telling me to do. My brain is able to process things more clearly when I am not being bombarded by other people's anger and when I am not using mental energy to come up with an opinion on everything. The world really doesn't need more opinions; what we need are people living their lives like they believe that God is real and that our souls will be judged on how we treat others. That is what I want to do. I know that everything is bad without social media telling me about it. I know racism is real, and I use every ounce of privilege that I have to make space for people who are kept out of places. I know that people need hope and support, and I try to make my work be something that gives them that. But I cannot do any of those things if I am allowing social media to drain my energy and make my thoughts toxic.

Social media is a tool. I've talked a lot about how much it hurts us, but none of us would have joined it in the first place if it didn't provide us with something good. I have met a lot of great people on social media. Social media helped give me the opportunities that led to this book. The best way to know if we are using it in a way that is helpful rather than harmful is to ask ourselves, Do I feel better after spending time on my social media, or do I feel worse? There is a practice called discernment that has been very useful to me in determining whether my time on social media is helpful.

Which, for the most part, it isn't, and how much I hate social media yet am still on it is proof that I am addicted to it.

When it comes to discernment and social media, I try to pay attention to what a post does for me. Does it give me hope and/or energy? Does it give me ideas? Does it give me something to write about? And if I am going to write, is what I am writing snarky and angry or inspiring and hopeful? Because when something on social media constantly makes me feel angry or hopeless, then I need to unfollow. If I feel drained and like the life has been sucked out of me, then I have been on social media too long and it is time for a break. If what I am writing is always an angry response to someone else, then I need to reevaluate what I want from my writing. Do I want to create more anger, or do I want to help build peace and justice?

So what do we do? I think we have to keep an eye on ourselves. Are we letting social media control our life? Are we scrolling until we are stressed out, feeling hopeless, and/or raging? Are we using social media as a means, or is it the end? Do we feel depleted when we scroll? Are our feeds things that nourish us, or are they answering a need that could be fed in another, better way? Social media can overwhelm us with anger, snark, insults, and ugliness, but it can also be a tool to share our story, to witness, and also to help others. We get to choose which one it is.

# 10.
# NOBODY GOES LIVE WHEN SH*T HITS THE FAN

I began using social media on MySpace, and that was back when dinosaurs roamed the earth in internet years. Since then I have seen a lot of things change with social media. I have seen how picking your top ten friends can be used as a way to let people know they pissed you off, and my two best friends and I have deleted and refriended each other at least twenty times since the MySpace days.

Instagram has been a whole other beast, though. It is my favorite social media app, but it is also the most dangerous for me, because it has me comparing myself to others the most. I see perfectly curated pictures of people living their best lives or getting to go on vacation or buy another house or have a house with a pool or a horse or they have the perfect hair or perfect eyebrows . . . the list of comparisons is endless. There are moments when every single picture or story I see on that app has something in it that I wish I had.

But in therapy I discovered that I am comparing two realities. It would be easy for someone to look at my Instagram feed and assume untrue things. In fact, people do that all the time. For example, they assume that because I announced the publication of this book that I am now rich. If I told you how untrue that is and gave you solid numbers on how much money Catholic writers make, you would die. We make nothing. This is truly a labor of love, and to be honest, I sometimes don't love it at all.

The truth is, there is so much space between the picture and the caption and real life. Not because everyone is fake, but because who goes live when they hate their husband? Nobody whose relationship is even a little bit healthy. Everyone gets into ugly fights with their spouse, kids, the neighbor, the chick who cut you off on the highway, or the lady at Starbucks who refuses to stop yelling at you through the intercom. Those things happen in real life. You get into a car wreck, you somehow did not budget correctly and now you are facing a disconnect notice from the light company, your child won't stop peeing in the bed, or the dog humps your leg all the time. Whatever it is that goes on in your real life that you can't post on social media is happening in everyone's real life, and they are also not posting it on social media. We are all posting our best moments or our deepest reflections months or years after the hard stuff. So we can all just stop comparing our real life with the bits and pieces of everyone else's life that we have a window into.

As I am writing this book, something happened in my family that I cannot share on social media. I have talked to my support system about it and gotten advice from them; I made an appointment to see my therapist too. But what I did not do was go on social media and tell everyone about it. We all have things that we cannot share, both current and past. I am an oversharing person, and even I have those things. And when we are healing from both generational trauma and past trauma, we will have a lot of moments that we don't feel ready to share. It takes a long time for things to end up where you feel comfortable talking about them and your healing from them. That does not mean that the work you did and are doing or the wisdom you are gaining from that work is worthless. I still have to show up in my work and do what I am called to do even though there is so much still left in me to heal. This is not failing; this is healing. So many times I have been tempted to stop sharing what I feel comfortable telling others about because it makes me feel like a fraud. I know there is still so much mess to clean up.

The truth is that I am doing what I can to handle each crisis as it comes. I have learned a lot of lessons from the way I have lived my life, and that is what I am sharing for anyone who can get something out of it. I tell my story so that people who think they are failing can see that healing is a process and a long one at that. It is normal to still have pain and hurt to work through, but that does not mean the things you have learned and wisdom you have gained are not valid.

That brings me to sharing about my son's suicide. From the beginning I told people exactly what happened. I started posting about it even as his body was still lying on the garage floor. The reason is that I did not want shame to control the

narrative of Anthony's life and death. I am proud of that
choice because suicide can create a huge cloud of shame. I
have never been ashamed of Anthony in my life, and I was
not going to start being so because of how he died. He is not
his suicide. He is Anthony. I created space to share our story,
my grief, and Anthony's life. And it made space for others
to share their stories. So many times in suicide loss, people
feel like they cannot talk about what happened and so they
don't. That creates room for the whispers. I knew this, and
I did not want that for Anthony. So I told everyone what
happened from the beginning.

Part of why I shared was also shock. When I typed out,
"Today, Anthony took his life" on Facebook, I was not in a
place where those words were real. They had not sunk in.
It was still all very much an alternate reality. But because I
typed them, I had to accept them. I do not think everyone
has an obligation to act in the same way when it comes to
their own trauma or suicide loss. Everyone gets to choose
for themselves what they do and how they tell that story, but
for me, I had to share the story in a way that was truthful to
the best of my ability.

This is also why I share about my childhood sex abuse. It
is how I take back what was taken from me. It is how I give
people permission to tell their stories also. But when I have
a sweat-drenching nightmare, I'm not going to Instagram.
I'm going to therapy. That is not me being fake or lacking
in "realness"; it is me taking care of myself. And that goes
for everyone sharing whatever it is they feel they are called
to share online. Every single one of our lives is a mix of joy,

things falling apart in the worst ways possible, and our call to do God's work.

# 11.
# KIDS CAN DO THEIR OWN LAUNDRY

I talk to a lot of mothers who are overwhelmed. We get so many messages from all over the place on what we should be doing or not doing, how we should be hustling but drinking water and also having a good time at wine o'clock but being present in our children's lives and also making sure we get our hair, nails, and feet done and also working out so that we can stay hot and do hot girl things. We are supposed to do *all* of this, and men are just supposed to go to work and maybe make pancakes on Sunday. This is why we are overwhelmed, both the amount of stuff we are expected to do and the number of messages we get as women that contradict each other. How do we take care of ourselves while also making sure our hair and makeup are done and we're working at least forty hours a week plus cooking dinner every night? It's crazy.

Women tend to juggle many more things at one time than men. Also, as Jen Fulwiler likes to point out, we were not meant to do life alone and isolated in suburbia. But so many of us are. We are meant to have community. I am so lucky that as a woman of color this is obvious to me. My son was born into a family community. My cousins and I all helped each other with our kids. If one baby needed a diaper change, then we changed all the babies at the same time. We all cooked something for dinner and met at someone's house to eat. That is how my family operated; we did things collectively. This is not how American culture, and especially white American culture, thinks of life.

Eventually, I traded that community for the suburbs and thought that I had "made it." But in reality, I was isolated. I ended up with all the responsibilities of a household on my shoulders. I worked as a waitress around all of the kids' schedules, and on top of that dealt with cleaning the house, cutting the grass, and all the other chores that come along with having a home and family. And then I was in a new marriage and had to make time to spend with my husband, who was busy with his own job and responsibilities. I now work forty hours a week in an office, and I understand why American women who work full-time and juggle all these responsibilities are at the end of their ropes.

Looking back, I realize I parented from guilt. I have a lot of guilt still. It's hard not to have guilt between all the things pulling at your attention and the trauma you carry around with you, but that doesn't mean it has to affect your parenting. Parenting from guilt does not do you or your child any favors. It does not give them what they need, and it does not help them learn how to set boundaries, keep their word, or take care of themselves, which all adults have to know how to do unfortunately.

My way of parenting was also driven by a desire to not be my mom. I never wanted my kids to do chores because my mother was a clean freak, and I hated helping her clean the house when I was little. I know now that so much of what I thought my mom did wrong was really me blaming her for a lot of my trauma as a child. I realize that I was wrong in that. My mother did the best she could with the resources she had. She was a great mom and wanted me to be safe. But for so long I thought if I just did the opposite of what she did, I would be a better mother than her and my kids would not have any trauma. So my kids never had to clean their rooms, eat their vegetables, or do their homework. None of these were priorities for me. I wanted them to respect me and be good people. When we became Catholic, I wanted them to go to Mass and their catechism classes. I don't even know why I expected or didn't expect things from my kids other than I just did not want to be my mother. Because she made me do chores, and because the chores allowed me to be abused, I did not make my kids do the things that would have been good for them to do.

It was not until my youngest son was about ten and the oldest sixteen that I began making them do their own laundry. (I might have these ages wrong, between my brain fog and old age, I'm not sure. It was some time between the one-story house and the two-story house.) The protest was

real. They all acted like I was the worst mom ever and that
I had abandoned them. But eventually, it was just the way
it was, and I was free from the never-ending laundry pile. I
was also free from being asked to buy them more clothes. It
was a win-win. But because I didn't want the kids to resent
me and the chores, I never did get around to them fully
taking on a set of chores that could help relieve me with
the housework. When I was going to start working on that,
Anthony died. And then the rest of my kids were out of the
house, and the time for figuring out chores was gone. So all
I have is insight from what I did wrong, not what I did right,
with my kids. My grandkids are a different story. What I have
learned with my grandkids is that children want to be a part
of their family and community. They want to be treated
like people and not just kids who get told what to do. If you
talk to them, they will do chores. If you badger them, are a
dictator, or insult and humiliate them, then you get me. Part
of being in a family is to help; that is also how we show up
in our community. It is almost as if God gave us our families
to learn how to live in community. Interesting: He seems to
have a plan for how this is all supposed to come together, if
only we paid more attention.

Chores cannot be about control or power but about
teaching. Teaching your kid how to do laundry and dishes
is a life-skill lesson. For the longest time, I thought parenting
was about control. But chores are not about proving that
you are stronger than them or that you can make them do
something. Chores are certainly not about them meeting
your expectations to prove that they are worth being loved.

From the moment your child is born, they are closer and closer to moving out of your house and living on their own in society. Do society a favor and please send out stable human beings. Being a parent is being a teacher.

You know your kids; you know what their gifts are. Work with their talents and gifts to come up with a system that works for everyone. That means both making them do chores and also figuring out how to spend time with them so you aren't drowning in guilt about how little time you spend with them. Having happy kids is not a sign that you are spoiling them; it is a sign that you are parenting them well.

Kids are not our possessions, and we are not their house-keepers or private chefs. We are all human beings in rela-tionship with one another. When they are young, we are responsible for their well-being and for helping them learn to navigate the world. We do not have to make sure they are perfect, so that the person who sits behind us at church thinks we are good parents. Our children are not reflections of our goodness. They are people. And one day they will be free to make their own choices, even choices that we do not agree with. Even choices that are dangerous. Even choices, when they are parents, that are exactly the opposite of what we did. Even choices that make the lady who sits behind us at church think we are bad parents. Who cares?

When Anthony died, I felt that everyone was going to think of me as a bad mom because my kid died by suicide. In the end, it doesn't matter what anyone thinks. It is easy to pass judgment on others, but at the end of the day, our judg-ments do not matter. What I have learned since Anthony's suicide is how much of my mothering was wrapped up in making sure that other people thought I was a good mom. That is what I based my expectations of my kids on, not on their ability to pay their own light bill or do their laundry when they moved out of the house. I spent my time trying to prove myself to some imaginary stranger instead of building relationships with my children by teaching them things they would need in life.

If there is one thing I wish I could do over, it is parenting my children. From beginning to end, I would do things so differently. I would know that using my kids as some kind of measure of my goodness is way worse than making them clean the house. I would know that avoiding parenting them because of guilt is way worse than just parenting them. When my children were young I had all my priorities messed up, but I don't get another chance with them. All I can do is write this, hope that someone with little kids gets something out of it, and do better as I help with my grandkids.

You do not have to do it all alone. You do not even have to have a community to help you, although that would be great. But what you can do is create community in your home and with your kids. Instill the idea in your family community that we are all in this together and we can all pitch in to do things. This will help them later in life when they are adults and have their own families. Maybe that is how we build community—first between us and our children, and then we let that community spread. But we do not have to set ourselves on fire to keep everyone warm. We do not have to do all the work ourselves. We can all gather firewood and help build the fire to keep us warm, whether by relying on our community or by making a family community where that group work is normal.

# 12.
# LAVENDER IS THE NEW DRUG

I love lavender. It's pretty, it's calming, and it's better than Grey Goose. Grey Goose does not work for me anymore because I no longer drink to numb myself from pain, but lavender is a great replacement. The problem is trying to find lavender essential oils without activating the MLM (multi-level marketing scheme) moms. Even if you don't know the term, you know what I'm talking about: the people you haven't talked to in nineteen years who suddenly want to "reconnect" on social media. Friendship should not be about extracting money, follows, or "connections." Maybe some of us have even begun to see our friendship with Jesus this way. Jesus won't buy your lavender either.

When I scroll Facebook or TikTok, I see a lot of people talking about self-care, therapy, and healing from trauma and generational wounds. I have had to learn all of these things for myself because I come from generational poverty and trauma and a long line of women who were never cared for and never learned how to take care of themselves. The women in my family line were taught to light themselves on fire to keep everyone around them warm. That was handed down to me.

Being the one on fire means feeling bitter and resentful when everyone around you keeps asking what's for dinner, complaining about how you do more for so-and-so than for them, and not once wondering if you might need a bucket of water or some burn cream. People are cold, and so we pour gasoline on ourselves and set the match, hoping to God that someone comes to our rescue or at the very least has some sympathy for us. The truth is, nobody ever does. And many times they will say, "Well, you lit yourself on fire; that's not my fault." Only it will sound more like, "She won't mind dealing with that cranky customer; she always takes care of them for us," or "Of course we can rely on her to volunteer! She always does!"

For generations, members of my family lived in survival mode. The women weren't taught to ask for what they needed because often it was simply not possible to get. My family members struggled even for food and other basic needs, so everyone just learned to survive. They didn't stop to think about asking someone else to deal with something while they rested; there's no time for that in survival mode. They didn't check with themselves about what kind of self-care they needed; they just set themselves on fire. To this day, if I say "self-care" to my mother she will die laughing and then cuss a lot in Spanish.

At one point in my life I was the most selfish mother on the planet, even though I couldn't see it as selfishness. I was working double shifts waiting tables or bartending, sometimes doing both a double shift waiting tables and then bartending until 3 a.m. Although I talked a lot about not letting anyone hurt my kids, it was me who hurt them the most. That is, it was my choices that put them in situations to be hurt—from the choice of who their fathers were to my choice to chase men when I could have been at home taking care of them. All of it was caused by my idea that after working so hard to provide for them, I had the right to have fun, live my life, and do what I wanted. After all, my kids were home safe with my mom, who fed them and made sure they took a bath and had clean clothes to go to school. The things I read reinforced this attitude and said I didn't have to give up myself and my life to be a mother; I had every single right to be me. And so I was. I centered my life on me.

This resulted in a lot of damage. My children, like me, are now stuck with having to heal from their own childhood trauma. And until a certain amount of healing occurs, some of that damage will continue to impact our relationships today. The hurt my choices caused my children will always be my greatest regret.

After spending time in therapy and working to face my faults and make changes in my behavior, I have found that the hardest part of my healing process is balancing self-care with my responsibilities as a mother, wife, daughter, and MayMay. (This is what my grandkids call me. I am not a grandmother, I am a MayMay, and if you do not have one,

you are really missing out!) At some point in my healing
process, I gave up the Grey Goose numbing method and
replaced it with the religious numbing method. Both are
distractions from looking at the hard stuff and dealing with
it. Neither is self-care.

When I became Catholic, I jumped in feet first. I went to
daily Mass. I ran out of my house at night yelling at my kids
that I had to go to the pregnancy center to help a mother in
a crisis situation, and they would have to take care of themselves for dinner. The irony in that sentence is not lost on me.
I neglected my children in order to take "pro-life" action.
First, my children had no time with me because I was out
working or drinking, and then that flipped upside down and
they had no time with me because I was doing all the pious
life things. Really, both of these were just ways for me to try
to feel better instead of actually facing my issues and working
to heal them. And this is what I see people do with all kinds
of things: essential oils, CrossFit, different diets and lifestyles.
None of these things are wrong, but we may wrap ourselves
up in them to avoid the hard truth of who we are, what has
been done to us, what we have done to others, and how to
confront and process it all; not to mention make reparation.

It is easier to distract ourselves with lifestyles—the
crunchy lifestyle, the workout lifestyle, the homestead lifestyle, the essential oil lifestyle—than it is to face our own
sins. Eckhart Tolle said that the word *sin* means missing the
mark on love. Reading that line turned on a light bulb for
me and began my work of looking at all the ways I missed
the mark on loving others. And then I started looking at all

the ways that I missed the mark on loving myself. Self-care means taking care of yourself because you love yourself, and that mark is easy to miss when you do not see your full self: the self that needs healing, the self that believes she needs to sacrifice everything for others, the self that harms others, even the self that hides because she thinks she is too awful to look at.

After Anthony's suicide, I began an exhaustive plan of trying to figure out all the ways that I had caused him to kill himself. I was sure that the answer to his suicide was in the mistakes of my motherhood. With the help of my therapist, what I found instead was all the ways that I did the best I could under really bad circumstances. That perspective also extended to my mother, who did the best she could under even worse circumstances. From that place of grace for both myself and my mother, I could accept ownership of the things I did do and let go of the idea that I was responsible for Anthony's suicide.

Once I reached that point of healing, I found I could enjoy things for themselves rather than try to use them as a magic potion to cure the pain of my life. I could enjoy drinking a lavender latte without expecting it to fix the problems of the day. I could go to daily Mass and take in my time with God without thinking, *This is the box that I need to check to be "good" or better than others*. I could care about the dignity of the human person from womb to tomb without ignoring my own family members or being a jerk to others who disagreed with me. And I could take care of myself in healthy ways rather than self-medicate while neglecting my family and calling that self-care. I had dug through a lot of trauma and found myself, which let me own up to all the ways that I missed the mark on love. This gave me the opening to do a 180 and set about doing things in a different way.

By no means am I perfect now. I have so much more to do and so many more things to repair, but I am way further along than I was before. When I start thinking about the next best thing that is going to make all my wishes come true, I check myself. I read books about how to become a good writer, mother, or human while knowing that nothing is magic. Not even Jesus. Everything in my life requires something of me, but I no longer believe that I am worth something only if I produce something. There is a balance and nuance between those two things.

None of this is easy. It's not easy to learn how to stop setting yourself on fire for everyone or how to stop indulging every whim while calling it self-care. I still do those things at times. But now, I do not measure my success by how much money I make (which is probably why I'm broke) or how I take care of others or how I take care of myself, but rather by how healed I show up to the day. Some days I am a mess. But more days now I have shown up as my full self, flaws and all, and been happy about my life when I go to sleep.

# 13.
# THE G CODE

When I was in high school, I moved from rural Texas to a city and school whose population was majority Black. This was a huge culture shock for me because our school in my rural town had only three Black students from kindergarten to twelfth grade. That was it. When I showed up at my new school, I was pretty racist and didn't know it. I made faces at and was scared of the Black students. One day one of the star football players told me that I was going to get beaten up if I didn't get over myself. He became one of my closest friends and still is to this day. After that, I began to make friends and get to know people. Sometimes they would take me to their grandmas' houses. Everyone began to realize that I did not have a strong relationship with my family. I did not know my cousins very well and I was a real nerd. All I wanted to do was read books and ask questions.

I learned a lot from my Black friends who took me in and made me a part of their community. I learned about Tupac and Biggie and Mary J. Blige—so basically about good music. I learned about racism, Dr. King, and the fight for civil rights. I also learned lessons about racism in real time as I saw how my Black friends were treated at the mall. Once when we were walking home, the police stopped us and put my Black friends facedown on the hot summer asphalt and let me and another girl go. We ran to get their grandmothers. Luckily everyone got home alive that day. As I have watched the events of recent years unfold, since the murder of Michael Brown, I have thought about that day. I have thought about everything I've learned from my BIPOC friends and family—that is, Black, Indigenous, and People of Color. From my Black friends and their grandmothers to my great-grandmothers and my cousins.

The lessons of how not to gossip, not to cheat, to always be loyal to those who look out for you, and to be a ride-or-die kind of friend—all of these things make up what we called the G Code in my neighborhood. The G Code is not easy to explain; it is kind of a vibe. It means that you are not sketchy or flaky. There is a monologue in a Tyler Perry play where Madea, the main character that he styled after one of his aunts, says, "I put everyone in the category of a tree; some people are leaves."[2] She goes on to say that some people are limbs that break when you step on them, but then there are the roots of the tree, those people who are steady and provide support. The G Code is rootlike behavior. It means that you will never be the one to hurt someone you care about. That you will not hesitate to show up for someone.

The G Code is why I have faced the fact that I benefit from white privilege and that I can do more than just read books and educate myself. I can help make space for Black voices. I was at a conference once with a panel on how to give BIPOC a voice. There was one Latina on the panel and three white people who had adopted Black children. A woman stood up and asked the panel for practical ways that white people could give people of color a voice. I watched as these very nice woke white people passed the mic to each other scratching their heads until someone said, "Why don't y'all start by giving the Latina the mic." The most practical thing they could do to give a person of color a voice in that moment was right in front of them, but they couldn't see it until it was pointed out to them. I laughed about that situation for hours after it happened. But it was the G Code that opened my eyes as a teenager to my own racism, allowing me to become an adult who could see it.

It is also why I debated about whether to even write this chapter. Because there is a fine line between appreciation and appropriation. And I will tell you the God's honest truth, I played jump rope with that line for a very long time. I even went on Facebook several times and ranted about hating the word *appropriation*. I would much rather hand this chapter over to a Black woman to write, but it is not just up to Black women to dismantle racism when they are not the ones who built it. So I can only tell you my own story. The story of how Black people took me in and taught me how to be a better person, how not to lie because someone will always have proof of what really happened, how to always stick up for your friends and they will always stick up for you and if they don't then walk away from them because they are not your friends, and how to just overall not be a jerk. Or a racist. And when you are, to correct yourself.

People ask me all the time why I am always making room for Black voices; I even made a website called *Catholic Speakers of Color* to help promote the voices of Black Catholics. The answer is that they deserve to be heard. And anyone who is shutting them out is missing out on some good things. Nobody can give you lessons on how to hope better than someone who lives in a country built to keep them from being seen as human beings. Not that it is Black people's job to give us hope, but it is our job to listen to their voices to understand what Black culture is without trying to take it for ourselves.

And no, this is not about being woke. This is about love. This is about justice. This is about the Gospel that says we are all made in the image of God. If we think that Black people are less than human—or if we act like that even when we would never say it—then we are calling God a liar. This is about the Catholic Church's teaching on the sin of racism. This is about how the Ten Commandments *are* the G Code. That is what blew my mind when I became Catholic—that what I was learning about how God wants us to love each other was stuff I already knew.

I had this epiphany one night during RCIA, when Noe handed out a paper that he called "an examination of conscience." On that paper were little sins like *do not gossip* and *do not lie*. And I realized I knew this list. This was the G Code. The people in my neighborhood knew these things because they knew truth. The truth that we are all created to know instinctively.

All of us know that we gossip for the sake of feeling better than someone else or to distract from our own flaws, but it does not feel good or wholesome when we are doing it. In fact, there is this fear of being seen for who we are so we would rather put the attention on someone else, and that is where the juicy "Did you hear about what happened?" comes in. What the G Code taught me is that there is something more important than being better than everyone else: being real. That means flaws and all. That required me to trust that I was safe to be myself with the people around me. And it also taught me to be brave enough to tell someone to their face if I had an issue with them. These were things that were required of me to be in this community.

Likewise, that is what the Ten Commandments are all about. They are about living in a community of human beings and watching out for all the ways that we could harm that community if we do not pay attention. The examination of conscience is how we pay attention. The fight for justice requires us to tell the truth and to confront things head-on, but to do so with love and without disrespecting the dignity of the person we are confronting. It is a very tight rope to walk, and God knew that, so he gave us help. Part of the help God gave me was the Black community where I went to high school. They loved me and took me in. They gave me the freedom to be myself while holding me accountable when I messed up. That is the same thing that Catholicism does for me and for all of us. Our faith invites us in, gives us freedom, holds us accountable, and in the process, it shows us how to fight for justice and love the people around us.

# 14.
# CUSSING IS NORMAL

I cuss like a sailor. Looking back, I see that it all started when my mom forbade me to listen to my favorite song when I was seven or eight. It was "Funky Town," and my mother, who speaks Spanglish as her everyday language, thought the lyrics were "F*ck It Town." Ironically, if that was true, it would still be my favorite song now. My mom also did not allow me to say "shut up" or "punk," which was really awkward because Punky Brewster was my role model as a child. I found all of these restrictions on words to be annoying especially because I had already been told I could no longer speak Spanish.

I was born in 1977 to a mom who was thirty-five years old and single. Well, she was married but separated, and that marriage was probably not legal since the man she married had another wife in Mexico, but either way, he was not my dad. My dad was nowhere to be found when I was born. My mom is the most innocent type-A rule follower that I have ever met in my life. She does not drink, smoke, cuss casually in English (Spanish is a whole other matter), or take naps.

I think maybe in the last five years she's gotten a little less anti-nap, and she took a Jell-O shot with my son Daniel for his twenty-first birthday. But still, she is a square. She began working in the fields when she was four years old and has worked every day of her life since. She is eighty years old now and is barely beginning to enjoy her life.

My mom was not my grandfather's biological child, but he raised her and she loved and respected him as her father. And that meant that she did everything he told her to do. He was Tejano and had very clear values and expectations. My mother accepted that. He was a good man, he worked hard to provide for his family, and he loved his children. My grandmother was what would probably be diagnosed now as bipolar, and he just rolled with it. My mother was the oldest and was expected to fill in the gaps created by her mother's mental health issues and trauma, which is something that somehow got passed down to me when I was a kid.

My mother was a shy child who was bullied in school for the few years she went. At the time schools were segregated, and the Hispanic/Mexican/Tejano kids all went to the white school, which was not a good thing for those kids. They were bombarded with racial slurs, and at one point, some white students cut off my mother's braids and threw her face-first in the mud. That was the last time she went to school. Instead, she went to work in the fields. She was in the third grade.

The most scandalous thing my mother ever did was get pregnant with me out of wedlock. She went big, I guess. She didn't cuss, drink, or smoke, but she got knocked up by someone who was not her husband. And that is the tiny part of my mother that I am exactly like.

I am telling you all of this because this is a huge reason that me and my mom do not get each other. My mother likes rules. She is a rule follower. Had she not had the trauma of living in poverty, facing racism, and dealing with dysfunction from a parent with undiagnosed mental health issues, she would have been a great student because she liked doing what was expected of her. I, on the other hand, hate rules. I do not follow them unless I have teased out every possible option and researched why *this* is the way to do something.

So when my mother told me that I could not do something, I was for sure going to find a way to do it. I felt that she was the prison warden I had to get by to do anything fun, including swearing. So from the first moment I found myself with nobody watching me, I started dropping f-bombs like there was no tomorrow. Before I knew it, I was in the fifth grade and I just started cussing one day at recess. I remember the silence of the other kids, and I didn't care. From that moment on, it was the sailor life for me.

In high school I moved from my small rural town to a city eight hours away. In most places that would be another state altogether, but I am from Texas, where you can drive for sixteen hours and never leave the state. So I went from a small cow town with four thousand people to a big cow city with several hundred thousand people. We moved into a neighborhood next to the Black community, and my high school was considered the "Black school." This is when I really learned how to use bad words as slang. And I never looked back. Cuss words just became part of my vernacular. And I didn't care who was offended by it. It was how I and my friends talked. End of story.

Then, after decades of swearing, I became Catholic. In my mind, that meant I had to stop cussing. In the months after my conversion, I made up my mind that that meant I had to stop being me. There was a list of things that I felt were not acceptable about me if I was going to be a "good Catholic." The biggest thing on that list was cussing. I had to stop saying bad words. And I had to stop offending everyone when talking to them because I cussed so much. It also created this idea of me that people carried and shared with each other. So I did. I stopped cussing, and I went to Confession about it over and over when I messed up.

One day I watched a comedy special by Anjelah Johnson where she has this bit about how Christians gossip and disguise it as prayer requests. I laughed and laughed, but then I thought about the truth of that. I thought about all the ways that I had seen nice suburban women dehumanize others politely and without a single cuss word. I began to talk to God about this in prayer and to discern what language was for. I was also processing the fact that for me, language had an element of trauma. One day when I was a small child I was no longer spoken to in Spanish or allowed to communicate in the only language that I knew. In rebellion, I began cussing.

In all my praying, processing, and reading about language, what I concluded is that there are plenty of ways that we dehumanize each other without using cuss words. There are many vulgar words that polite people use, that are not on the list of "bad words." I thought about how intention is the key to how we use words. What am I communicating, and who am I communicating it to? What is my mood when I am communicating it? Because if I am super salty and angry, I can still tell people off using nice words. We see on memes and on TikTok how office culture has an entire language to communicate displeasure in polite but passive aggressive ways. What is more important, not cussing or being honest and charitable?

Being charitable is a lot harder than simply not cussing or using the right tone. It is about examining ourselves and being honest about the message we are conveying. When I examine myself, I see that more often than not my intention when I am angry is to hurt the person I am angry with. And I can cause that hurt with all kinds of words; the words are not what matter, but the intention behind them.

I was once driving down the highway with my oldest son. I said, "You freakin' dumb bunny!" to a car that cut me off, and Anthony told me, "That is just as mean as if you said, 'go eff yourself, asshole!'" I rolled my eyes. Then later that day a very "nice" woman in a Facebook group insulted me. When I cussed her out, I was the one who was kicked out of the group because in the eyes of the person in charge, I had been the rude one. It did not matter that her words, while not cuss words, had been just as hurtful to me as my cuss words were to her. And that is when I could feel God smirking at me as if to remind me of the conversation I had had with Anthony in my car during traffic. I ignored him.

Which is what I do when God smirks at me. It doesn't get me very far in life, but I keep refusing to learn that lesson.

Then there was the time that I tried to avoid cussing, and I found myself insulting people with nice words that were full of disdain. Again, God made me see how it is not always about what words we use but rather the intent behind them. I can be hurt and hurt others with strings of sentences that do not have a single cuss word in them, or I can drop twelve f-bombs while complimenting my best friend. No, I shouldn't go around disrespecting spaces and the people around me by cussing, but more than that, I have to check myself on what I am saying and what my intention is. Even if, on paper, what I'm saying seems perfectly nice.

Knowing this changed how I looked at hurting others with my words, whether my words were gossip masked as a prayer request, me actually looking out for someone's best interests, or me insulting someone to their face in a way that wasn't obvious. And I stopped worrying about whether I was cussing because really all that did was give me an out so I didn't have to examine how I was treating others. For me, not cussing was a way to pretend I was being charitable without actually confronting the motive behind my words.

In the end, we need to make sure that we are using loving and grace-filled language when we talk to other human beings. When we focus on a list of "bad words" we are or are not using, that just lets us off the hook from digging deep into how we are really showing up in our conversations and our relationships. Even our relationship with God. Yes, I use cuss words in my prayers sometimes. I never cuss *at* God, but I do sometimes cuss when I am talking to him because that is just me being honest. He would much rather us show up honestly than with fake piety when he knows who we are. That is the same way I try to show up in all my relationships. Honestly.

# 15.
# HOLINESS IN DIVE BARS

I have learned more about Jesus at bars than anywhere else. I began working in a dive pool hall during the lunch shift when I was eighteen. I had worked as a cashier in a Mexican food place in Amarillo, Texas, and my cash register was right behind the bar. I watched these supercool human beings flip drink shakers as they laughed and charmed their customers. It looked like a fabulous existence. So I began to daydream about the day that I could wear one of the sharp all-black uniforms and work behind the bar too.

Instead, I ended up doing the day shift at a pool hall down the street. It was boring in the beginning because nobody plays pool at 10 a.m. I was in charge of weighing the bottles and checking in inventory. It took me a minute, but eventually I figured out the routine. I got in around 10 a.m., opened up, weighed the bottles, and set the bar up, and then the barflies would start coming in looking like whiskey zombies. All of them looked like they had died three days before, and the bar would be silent until the beginning of the third round of drinks. That is when someone would finally play the first song on the jukebox. It was usually Lynyrd Skynyrd's "Sweet Home Alabama." All of a sudden the people at the bar came to life. And that is when I learned the most valuable lessons of my life. (It is also when I learned to smoke and drink like a fish.)

Those barflies taught me about not giving up on people. And what community means. It means being in common union with other human beings who see past your flaws or do not even see them to begin with. When one of these guys got sick, the rest would pitch in to send them a card or help with groceries. If someone went on vacation, they told everyone so none of us would worry when they didn't show up at the bar.

These men, all of them in their late fifties or early sixties, taught me how to defend myself if I was being harassed. They defended me themselves if it happened before 6 p.m., which is when they went home after a full day of drinking. I also learned to read the paper because, every single morning, the first bit of conversation was about what was in the newspaper that morning and everyone had their opinion about it. It was the way Instagram is now, only in person and with real conversation. Also, if you were a troll, you would get your ass kicked out.

The main thing that I learned from these regulars was how to laugh even in the middle of the awfulness of life. Even though they probably had a serious struggle with drinking considering they spent almost every day at a bar like it was a full-time job, they had a sense of humor. They taught

me how to tell stories because storytelling is the main enter-
tainment in a dive bar. I have loved storytelling my entire
life, and these people helped me to get better at that craft
and showed me how to tell stories honestly.

The honesty they had about who they were was the holi-
est thing I ever saw. It was the Church that I had heard
about my entire life but had not really seen in action. They
showed up every day as themselves and not as some fake
version of who they were. They did not deny their struggles
or the many ways those struggles impacted their lives but
they accepted themselves as they were. I now show up to
my prayers with that same kind of commitment to honesty
about myself. I do not hide from God. He already knows
who I am, what my failings are, and where I struggle. So
why hide it? I show up at the confessional the way those
men showed up at the bar every day: with honesty and like
it's my job.

I feel most at home in a dive bar. When I walk in, there's
no whisper in the back of my head that I don't belong the
way there is when I walk into other places. I can talk to anyone sitting at the bar; I can listen to their stories and tell my
own. I laugh, cry, and overshare about things that strangers
probably have no business knowing about me. Behind a dive
bar slinging drinks, I never question myself. I know who I
am and what I am doing. I do not ever question if I'm good
enough. I know that I'm the best bartender there is. That
kind of confidence is something that doesn't follow me once
I step out from behind the bar.

In 2001 I got fired from my job at Hooters, and I needed to work. I answered an ad in the newspaper for a job at a bar named Club Baloo. It was a new club in town in the same building where I had gone dancing on the weekends with my family when I was eighteen. Now I was married with four kids, and I needed a job. They hired me, and after a few months, a new guy started and was the bartender next to me. His name was Homer. I called him Homie. I was a jerk to him for months because he had the same name as Anthony's biological dad. He would clean the entire bar and mop the floor every night. He let me take all the customers, and I refused to split tips so he usually walked away with a quarter of the money that I had. But he never complained, he kept being nice to me, and eventually he became my best friend. We ended up working at another place together, and we would work all day and then go out drinking afterward. I could tell him anything. Not once did Homie ever hit on me or try anything with me. He defended me to his friends, and he never judged anything I did even though I did a lot of really judgeable things. Those things included going home with a guy I met at a bar when I went out with some other friends after my divorce. A few weeks later my gas was shut off because I hadn't paid the bill, and the guy from the gas company that came to shut it off was the guy I went home with. I didn't know his name and hadn't planned to see him ever again, and there he was in my backyard shutting off my gas.

Homie laughed hard when I told him that story, and he said, "Leticia, what you're looking for in men you can't find when you're sleeping with anyone who says your hair looks good. Everyone knows you can't turn a ho into a housewife." He said it in such a way and with so much kindness that I was not even offended. Instead I thought about what he said, and we talked more about it. Who I am now would disagree with a lot of the conversation we had that day, but it was the beginning of me looking at my actions and trying to figure out what I was doing and why I was doing it. I also realized that maybe I needed to change because I did not like who I was or what my life was. I brought my complete, honest self to my friendship with Homie, and because of that, he was able to support me when I needed it and also start to show me where I needed to change.

Then, on Cinco de Mayo in 2007, I lost him. Homie was out in the country with friends celebrating his birthday. He sent me a text asking me to go out with him, but I was staying home with Anthony at my house while my other kids were with my mom. I told him that I would go out with him the next night. I woke up the next day to a flurry of texts asking me what had happened to Homie and if I was OK. It took hours for me to track down someone who knew what had happened, and when I learned that he had been in a car accident and died, I lost it. I spent the next year drunk. I got kicked out of bars, I threw glasses at a bouncer who had beat up Homie the weekend before his death, and I was found drunk on bathroom floors. Finally, one day when I was being evicted from my house, I ended up lying on the grass in the front yard, asking God to let me die. I was tired.

A few weeks later I packed up everything in my car and got my kids from my mom's, where they had been staying while I tried and failed to pull myself together. Then I drove from Amarillo to Austin to start over.

I spent years floundering around in grief because I had no idea how to grieve other than to drink myself stupid. It was not until I was in therapy that I could really break apart that grief and see what exactly it was that I lost on the night that Homie died. I lost the first person who was safe for me. He did not ever hurt me. Up until I met him, every man I had been involved with had hurt me in some way, from big ways to little ways. But Homie was good to me. He never expected anything from me or for me to be any kind of way. He just accepted me. He was a good friend.

I also met my other best friend, Candie, at that bar. She liked a drink a certain way, a way that I did not make it, and she would return it over and over until I got it right. I hated her guts. How we ended up being ride-or-die friends is beyond me, but we have. She was with me the day I threw a fit at the funeral home demanding to see Anthony when the funeral director told me he was not ready. But it had been a week since I had seen him and he was in a cold box somewhere and I needed to see him. Candie looked at me and said, "Are we going to make a scene?" and when I nodded, she just said OK and we went in. And made a scene. We also got to see Anthony. She was on one side of me, and Stacey was on the other. But if it had not been for that bar, I would never have met her.

I have found holiness in bars in friendships like these and in the stories we share of the good times and the very worst things we have been through. Those friendships have taught me how to be in relationship with Jesus and share my full self with him. Those friendships have also taught me how to be in relationship with other people, how to love someone else and stand with them in their suffering and in my own. How to hear someone call me out for my dumb choices and think about their words rather than reject them. It is those friendships that have helped me to love myself, to look at my mistakes and still treat myself with love, like Homie did, rather than judgment.

I have found holiness in dive bars because that's where people are honest and real. And as he showed us over and over in the gospels, where people are honest and real about their brokenness, that's where Jesus meets them.

# 16.
# YOU ARE NOT A MACHINE

Listen, I am going to begin by repeating this one true fact about our faith: Jesus came to heal us. Sin wounds us, and some of those wounds carry down from generation to generation. I began my journey back to the Catholic Church through Oprah and her videos with Eckhart Tolle. As I mentioned earlier, Tolle talks about sin as missing the mark on love. In other words, sin is not an indicator that you are inherently bad. In fact, that you are capable of sin is proof that you are inherently good; otherwise, missing the mark on love would not be anything noticeable in your life. It would just be normal.

Thinking of sin as missing the mark on love helped me to uncenter myself in the story of sin and redemption. Sin is not only about me. It is so much easier to discern my sins when I consider them in light of love. Was this action loving to myself, to my husband, to my child, to my friend, to my mom? Or did someone miss the mark on loving me, and am I reacting out of how they didn't love me well? It is kind of like sorting laundry, and the reason I confess when I have missed the mark on love is to heal and to allow God to love me anyway. Confession isn't about being punished for what I did wrong; it's about getting healed so I can love others better.

This has led me to a very weird place of hating capitalism. Stick with me for a second, and if at the end of this you still don't get the connection and you want to write me off as a commie, then feel free. But I have thought about this for a long time because of who my mother is. My mom began working in the fields in the Texas Panhandle at the age of four. Unlike a lot of farmers, my mom did not own land or work land that her family owned. Instead, she worked someone else's land and that person paid her pennies. Literally. From the age of four, my mother was told that if she did not work and make money, then she was not valuable.

She has carried that belief about herself all of her life. Because she had to work, cook, and help with her younger siblings when she was a child herself, to this day she has to "do something" around the house to feel like she isn't a waste of space. And because she didn't know any better, she tried to instill that message in me. It sank in, but in a lot of ways it always seemed like a crock to me. I did not feel like my worth was based on how much money I had, how good I was at my job, or if my boss gave me a gold star for being the best employee. I wanted something more than money and work. I did not exactly know what I wanted, but I knew that there was more to my worth as a person than my ability to work and make money.

Work is holy. It is one way we commune with God. This is why St. Benedict's order is all about manual labor. There is nothing wrong with working for your living; what is wrong is being exploited by someone whose greed has made them see you as a walking wallet instead of a human being made in God's image.

Even worse than being exploited ourselves is when we decide the worth of someone else based on their usefulness to us. Or when we dehumanize someone who we think is low-class or somehow less because of what they do not have. Or when we think it is fine that kids go hungry because their parents should work harder. When we look at everything through the lens of value based on monetary worth, we lose a part of who God made us. We begin to see ourselves as machines who are only worth what our return on investment is. Human beings are not machines. We are not created by God only to work, sleep, and drive our kids to soccer games. We are created for relationships.

How we prioritize our time and set our boundaries is up to each of us. There is no one way that will work for everyone. I would like to think that everyone should do what my husband and I did and move out to the country to learn how to raise our own food and live off the grid. Even though I strongly believe that this is a great way to get in touch with how God created us, I know that God also made us all different. What works for me will not work for everyone else.

Our move has helped me feel closer to God and his creation. It has also taught me the difference between work and the exploitation of labor. Work is when we do things to nourish ourselves. These can be obvious things, like growing our own food or writing a book. One feeds our bodies and the other feeds who we are. Or they can be less obvious, like working in an office to buy our food or building homes to both earn money and grow the community. The exploitation of labor is when we work for the sake of making someone else's life comfortable and are not compensated appropriately for our time or effort.

To avoid exploitation, we must know who we are and what we want out of life and make sure that what is important to us is our priority. As long as we know that we are human beings and not machines, we can use every opportunity to be who God made us to be even when our situations aren't great. But we always have to be mindful that comfort and money are not what we are made for. We were created to be in relationship with God. To commune with him and to be in awe of him as he delights in us. We are created to live our lives well and to love and be loved.

Work is a good thing, and comfort can be good too. But when they become our main focus, we miss out on loving each other and letting God love us. And that is when work (if you're like my mom) or comfort (if you are more like me prior to our move) becomes a sin.

# 17.
# 2020

Or as I like to call it, "The Year the World Was Set on Fire."

In January of 2020 my husband was in Iraq as a contractor. One night while he was sleeping, he was alerted to get to a bunker because of incoming fire. While in that bunker, as Iranian missiles landed around him, he was notified from back home that the person he had considered his best friend for years had died by suicide. This happened as we were approaching the third anniversary of Anthony's suicide. My husband was the one who found Anthony and cut him down. And two months later . . . well, I think we all remember: COVID-19 lockdown.

While the beginning of the year was particularly hard on Stacey, once March hit, everything took a nosedive. For the most part, lockdown was not traumatic for me, my husband, my children, or my grandchildren. I had a good contracting job that was paying the bills, and Stacey was home from March until August. I was working from home, so we spent more time together than ever during those months.

We talked about everything and hashed out a lot of our conflicts. We spent days with our grandchildren running in the backyard. We were all safe in our house, and we had snacks in the pantry for the first time ever.

We were good.

That gave me perspective on a lot of things, especially on the people who weren't good. On Memorial Day weekend in 2020, in the middle of the pandemic, the world watched a viral video of a police officer murdering George Floyd, a Black man who was accused of trying to pass off a fake twenty-dollar bill. The video was horrific. For a minute, I felt that it was the one thing that would change the course of white supremacy in this country.

I have become more and more convinced that white supremacy is the devil incarnate, and I am not saying that to be dramatic. I believe this in a very spiritual and realistic way. And I've said this since the news of Ahmaud Arbery's murder—a murder that occurred earlier in 2020 but didn't become widely known until later that year—that this evil is fighting to stay in America. And none of this is new; it is a simple fact that Christopher Columbus, the man who "discovered" this country, fed Indigenous babies to his dogs and sold children into sex slavery. Then there is America's long history with chattel slavery.

How do we fight it? I think the secret is to not paint everyone with the same brush. This is also the hardest part. It is not easy to treat with kindness the people we strongly disagree with, but it is the only way. The devil wants to pit us against them because then he distracts us all, and honestly, if we destroy each other and ourselves in the process, then he has less work to do.

Times like this when people are in conflict and countries are trying to figure out how to move forward are the times when saints are made. Make no mistake, God makes people saints; we do not make ourselves holy by checking off boxes on how to be the best Catholics ever. So for me, I am ignoring the temptation to be mad at all the things happening in America and around the world and instead I'm working on what is in front of me. Not in a privileged "nothing bad is happening" kind of way, but in a humble "I can only do what God calls me to do and I am not the savior of the world, Jesus is," kind of way. I cannot fix everything. I can only fix my own sins and do what God asks of me. Right now, he is asking me to write this book, so as much as I want to burn things to the ground, this is what I am doing—working a full-time office job while writing a book and raising chickens for the first time. How it all fits together is really beyond me. I do know, though, that I am happy and I am helping others, using my gift of writing and filling my own soul with joy. There is no changing the world without changing myself.

The Catholic Church is my mother. When I was lost, she found me and healed me. I owe everything of who I am to her. But the people who are in this Church are not perfect. We have a lot of issues, but we also have the map of how to heal them. In our faith, we have the road to reconciliation down. We walk it every time we go to Confession.

When I was in RCIA, Noe told a story about a little boy who was playing baseball in his yard and accidentally broke his neighbor's window. He walked over to the neighbor and apologized and asked for forgiveness. The neighbor accepted the apology and forgave the boy, but the window was still broken and needed repair. That is the difference between forgiveness and reparation. How do we repair what has been broken? The need for reparation applies to our relationship with God, ourselves, and our neighbors, but it also applies to us as a Church and a society. How do we repair the broken windows we are responsible for?

The first step is always to acknowledge the harm we caused. I can imagine this is difficult for our bishops, who feel that they had no part in a lot of this. After all, they weren't even alive when Black people were enslaved in America, and it isn't their fault if police treat Black people different from white people. I understand this as someone healing from generational trauma. My great-grandfather was from Spain, and he won my Native American great-grandmother in a poker game. I don't know the details of their life together, but since this was the basis for their marriage and she ended up dying by suicide, I assume it was not a happy one. The trauma was passed down through generations even if the story of what life was like for her wasn't. I am trying to heal from the trauma I inherited, but I feel like a lot of damage has already been done to my own children. Their anger targeted at me seems unfair since many of our family's problems began way before I was born and I am also a victim of them. I feel like our bishops and priests must feel something similar. But we are the ones here when the pain is being uncovered . . .when the graves of Native children are being discovered and when my children are vocalizing generations of trauma. God put us here, and it is our responsibility to do the work to heal what we can.

The second step is to see how we benefit from the harm that we didn't cause and try to correct it. As a Hispanic Catholic, I know that I benefit from white privilege in a lot of ways. I also face racism regularly as a woman of color. I am married to a straight white male who is a redneck, and we have three half-white children. My oldest son was the grandson of a man who came to this country undocument-ed and was a deacon in the Catholic Church. Diversity is the brand of my family. So I use that to help anyone that I can. I use the space that I am given as a Hispanic woman to make space for Black women. I use the racism that I have faced and witnessed to confront the fact that racism is still alive and well in this country. I use the love I have for my husband and children to prevent myself from thinking that white people are evil; racism is. And I will die on the hill that it is the undocumented who are the most vulnerable in this country. Citizenship is a privilege.

The final step is simply to love. I learned all about lov-ing my neighbor from my childhood in Kenedy, Texas. I am a Native Texan, literally. I am Tejano. That means that my family has been Spanish, Mexican, Tejano, Texan, and American all without crossing any borders. My paternal great-grandmother was Indigenous and was born in San Saba, Texas, which is hours away from the Rio Grande

River. Because of colonization, borders crossed my family. But this land that is Texas is in my soul, and I love this state as much as anyone else, if not more. I grew up instilled with Texan values. We work hard, we take care of our own, we do not let anyone go hungry, and if someone needs something we can give them, then we give it to them without expecting anything in return. From the First Baptist Church, I also learned that Jesus loves me and that if I love him then I take his words seriously, I go to church, and God comes first. All of these things were drilled into me as a child in rural Texas where there were more cows than people.

Yet despite how all these good things were drilled into me as a child, 2020 gave me insight into the ways that I work with the forces of evil. Like when I flip off some stranger in traffic and my middle finger goes right past the crucifix on my rosary (that was laid on Jesus's tomb by the way, *yikes*) and I say something horrible. Or when I decide that someone is my enemy and obsess over every bad thing they do because I have to find reasons to prove that they should go to hell. Or when I point to how other people are in denial about their racism but gloss over the ways that I am also pretty freakin' racist. It is so much easier to point out the sins of everyone else than to sit with myself and admit my own. How exactly do we take responsibility for our part in social sins and also work on ourselves? It is a balance that I have not completely figured out.

But I do have a plan of action. I am going to show up to every single interaction with another person as myself and also with the intention of treating that person like they are made in the image of God. I cannot change anyone but myself. What I can do is give space to others who do not benefit from white privilege as much as I do while also fighting for justice and also showing up in spaces with people I disagree with and refuse to dehumanize them. And *all* of this comes after I prioritize my relationship with God. Because it is my relationship with God that leads to everything else I do.

The world is on fire. Working on my own sins and giving space to those who have been treated unjustly are ways that I can help put out the flames.

# 18.
# POPPING THE CATHOLIC BUBBLE

I believe in the power of storytelling. I love to hear people tell their stories, any stories, because I learn how they got to where they are both physically and spiritually. Part of my love for stories comes from working as a bartender. Part of it comes from spending a lot of time as a child in a nursing home. My mom was a certified nurses' aide, and she worked in a nursing home. If she did not have childcare, I went to work with her and sat in the dayroom with the residents, watching *Wheel of Fortune* or playing Uno with them. Let me tell you something: because of all my practice there, I can kill at Uno!

Old people enjoy telling their stories to anyone who will listen, and it just so happens that a five-year-old loves to hear stories. We made very good companions. I believe this is when the love of story was rooted in me. To this day if I find myself sitting with someone older than me, I ask if they've lived in this city their whole life in order to unravel the stories that they have stored in their hearts. Wisdom drips off of people older than me, people of a different race than me, people who have had different experiences than me, and people who have different opinions about life than me. I learn by listening to them.

As the years have gone by, I've lost the gift I had as a child of listening to stories without judging. Part of it is the current political climate. Some of it is my conversion to Catholicism that came with a certain vibe of those political opinions. It came with a certain arrogance on my part, thinking I had all the answers in becoming Catholic and anyone who did not see things the way I did was a moron. I have actually always been this way, but becoming Catholic and having a bubble to live in didn't help.

It was only after reading Elizabeth Scalia's book *Strange Gods* that I began to see myself dancing around the idol of "I am right and you are a moron," aka pride.[3] I took a hard look at myself and saw that I had alienated many people who loved me and who I pushed away with my snark and sharp words. And it would not be the last time that I saw this face looking back at me. I see that face again and again.

When I find a new cause or learn something new about the world, I jump in feet first. I make it the center of every conversation, and I buy forty-seven books on the subject. I do this because I love learning—absolutely love it. I love when dots connect and suddenly something that I have always felt to be true has a name. Learning is a gift. Loving knowledge and wanting to know more is something gifted to me by God. Where I ruin it is in my pride of thinking that because I now know something, it is up to me to change the world and save everybody.

In that, I am a lot like St. Peter. I say the wrong thing. I am wise enough to know who Jesus is, and then I cut the ear off some poor fool and Jesus has to tell me that I'm a big dummy for doing it. It has been an ongoing pattern all of my life. I am a ride-or-die person, and I ask no questions about where we are riding to and why anyone has to die. I just jump in. It is a very loyal thing, but it is also how you end up halfway to Canada and you have no idea why.

More than pride, though, the greatest sin that my love of knowledge and deep loyalty leads to is othering people and making them my enemies. I use the coded language of whatever bubble I am in to describe "them" and then claim the label that my bubble says "we" are. I draw lines in the sand and decide which camp everyone I encounter belongs in: Protestant, Catholic, pro-life, pro-choice, whole life, consistent life ethic, Democrat, Republican, white, Black, anti-racist, too much, too little, and so forth. My survival instincts assess everyone I meet and put them into a category for my own protection. So everything about me, from my love of learning to my loyalty to my survival instincts, feeds into my "us vs. them" mentality. I feel safe in a bubble; like I have found my people.

But eventually, all bubbles have to pop.

My Catholic bubble popped when I began to ask questions about racism and immigration. And then I went further and asked about certain ideas that I encountered in the pro-life movement. At one point during a highly dramatic bill passing in Texas one summer, I was forced to sit with pro-choicers because I had been mean-girled by a big name in the pro-life movement. As I talked to the pro-choice women, I realized how much common ground there is between the two sides that truly seemed to hate each other that day. Both sides supported maternal healthcare, access to resources for mothers who found themselves in unplanned pregnancies, and sex education. Sure, we disagreed a lot on how to deal with those issues, but we all cared for and wanted to improve situations for women. I now think that it is in discussions with those who have differing opinions but a common goal of helping women that we can find a way forward. However, that is not what I saw that summer at the Texas capitol. It was awful, from the satanic chants to freak out the Christians to the Christian women making their children kneel and pray with them in the midst of the chaos in the rotunda.

Since that summer, things have only gotten worse, on this topic and so many other ones. So how do we find a way forward? A way to pop our bubbles? Especially the Catholic bubble?

When I want to pop the Catholic bubble for myself, I think about what Jesus did in the midst of drama and politics. He healed people, and he told stories. I think telling our stories is healing work for ourselves and for others. I know that it is in telling Anthony's story that I have healed. I get emails, texts, DMs, and comments from people who have heard me tell his story who say they are more healed because of it as well.

If we remain in our bubbles and do not hear the stories of people we other, then we miss out on some of that healing. If we do not take the time to patiently listen to someone expressing their pain, then we miss out on our healing and also stunt theirs. In the secular world, this is called trauma-informed listening. We do not interrupt or put in our own two cents, but we let a person talk freely and just listen. Sherry Weddell, the founder of the Catherine of Siena Institute and a leading voice on evangelization, calls this the trust threshold of evangelizing in her book, *Forming Intentional Disciples*.

When we reduce people to their opinions and encounter them with the agenda of changing their ideas, we dehumanize them and deny them their dignity as humans made in the image of God. When we encounter people as humans made in the image of God, then God can work in them through us, and it is none of our business what the outcome of that work is. To be his instruments, we have to leave the comfort of the Catholic bubble. I would say we might even have to pop it, which is the most uncomfortable thing to do. But it is what God calls us to do. Jesus certainly left his bubble by his incarnation.

The first step in leaving our bubbles is to stop thinking of people outside of them as our enemies. If we cannot do that, then we can start by loving our enemies and praying for those who persecute us (see Matthew 5:44). Then we can move on to listening to others tell their stories and asking questions rather than giving our opinions. It takes practice, and I admit that it is still not second nature to me. I am still working on popping my Catholic bubble. I probably always will be.

Jesus used very specific language; as God, he knew exactly what he meant when he told us to love our enemies. He knew that the enemies he was talking about were the people who opposed us. Yet he said that we were to love them. Love does not mean agree with or submit to. It means to take their well-being into consideration. It means that we do not other them, which is a form of dehumanizing them. It means that we understand that we are also sinners.

I used to rationalize my bubble by thinking that I was being countercultural. The truth is that there are a lot of cultures in our world; I now think of each of these cultures as bubbles. There is no "counterculture" because there is no one culture. Each community has its own culture, even each parish community that helps make up the universal Catholic Church community—which also has its culture. When we come out of our bubbles and meet people where they are without an agenda to change them, we grow. This is particularly important for Christians because we believe that every person is made in the image of God. When we get to know a person, we get to know God more. When we humanize someone enough to hear them out, whether or not we agree with what they are saying, we honor God. When we ask someone we disagree with to tell us more, rather than telling them how they are wrong and listing all our arguments on just how wrong they are, we see them as people that God made and loves. Our goal should be about understanding someone more than winning a debate.

I have to think of the person I disagree with as someone who has their own life experiences that have led them to their own conclusions, just like me. That is not easy for me because I want to be right. I want to think that I have done all the research and all the learning, and everyone else should just take my word for it. But that is me taking away the right of other people to learn and come to their own conclusions, and it is also prideful to think they have nothing to teach me.

In the end, my job is to live my life in a way that holds my relationship with God as my priority. That is a witness to people that I hope will help them come into an encounter with Jesus. Then God has to do the rest. My job is not even to bring people into the Church; that is *his* job. When I remember that, I am so much less of a jerk who thinks that I have all the answers. Instead, I can be a human being who listens to others who like me are made in the image of God.

One of the first lessons my therapist taught me is that there are no *shoulds*. There are just things we do and reasons why we do them, but nobody deserves to be *should* on, not even myself. *Should* denies grace and understanding. *Should* kills companionship. *Should* implies that I am God, and I am not. All I can do is walk with people as they make the choices they are free to make and love them in the process. That is what evangelizing is; it is not creating an exclusive bubble where people are told how they *should* think and be in order to be loved. Instead, it is about meeting people where they are and loving them like Jesus does.

# 19.
# PRAYING THE ROSARY LIKE A LOSER

When I was going to the First Baptist Church as a child, I was taught that Catholics were the anti-Christ. One time Pope John Paul II came to San Antonio, which is thirty minutes from my hometown, and the youth pastor warned us all that he was the anti-Christ and the proof was the upside down cross on his chair. It made sense to me as a tract-carrying Baptist child.

It was awkward that my Tio Roy and Tia Mary were Catholic. Not just kind of Catholic, but *real* Catholic. They went to Mass every Sunday. My Tio was a fourth-degree Knight of Columbus who cooked every year for their annual festival, and my Tia was a religious ed teacher and also a member of the Catholic Daughters. When I was thirteen, my cousin Norma got married in the Catholic Church, and I was her maid of honor. That wedding was the first time that I ever considered the fact that I could not receive

Communion, even though I was baptized Catholic as a baby. It was the first time that I was ever curious about anything Catholics did.

When I was growing up, pictures of Mary were in every house I walked into. My Tia Mary had pictures, paintings, and statues of Mary and all kinds of other saints all over her house. To this day they are there to greet me when I go to that house, even though my Tio and Tia have been dead for years. My mother and other tias also had pictures of Mary and rosaries all over the place as well. But because of what I was taught in the Baptist church, I judged them as statue worshippers. I believed that the Rosary was connected to all of that witchcraft.

When I began attending RCIA so I could get Stacey to marry me, I was prepared to shoot down the idea that Mary was anyone other than just a regular girl and to defend the idea that the Rosary was witchcraft. I was ready. I had been to RCIA once before when I was pregnant with Anthony . . . and I was kicked out for asking why Catholics worshipped Mary. Fast-forward sixteen years, and I was ready for the story to repeat itself. I was not just in disagreement about Mary, statues, and the Rosary; I was openly hostile about all of them. And I was ready to be hostile about them with this brand-new priest too.

I never got that chance because Fr. J did such a great job explaining the Mass and John 6 about the Eucharist. I was too stunned to argue about Mary or the Rosary. I was in a rabbit hole trying to figure out why, as a Bible-thumping child, I had never read a word out of John 6. When we eventually got to the Rosary and Mary, I was still wondering why I had never heard Jesus's words about eating his flesh.

Eventually, after a lot of arguing, research, and a trip to Rome, I decided to really become Catholic. I was not just going to get the sacraments and play the part to get married; I really believed that Jesus had given us this Church. While in Rome I stood at the tomb of St. Peter and could hear the words of Jesus, "On this rock I will build my church" (Mt 16:18). It (St. Peter's) is literally built on top of the apostle's grave. I saw Pope Benedict XVI up close as he passed by me in the popemobile during a Wednesday audience. In person he looks nothing like he does in pictures, and this allowed me to begin letting go of some of my anti-pope mentality. I learned that the popes were all in line, that you could trace them all the way back to St. Peter, which was kind of cool. I also learned that for 1,500 years, all Christians were Catholic. We are the OG Christians.

I read the *Catechism* twice front to back before getting confirmed. It was so beautiful, but I also did not understand a lot of it. I disagreed with plenty of it, but there is such a vast amount of writing in a two-thousand-plus-year-old Church that I began to dig and dig and dig until I eventually went to college to get a bachelor's degree in philosophy.

There is a huge gap between what I read and learned about Catholic teaching and what I see on social media paraded around as Catholicism. I see Catholics ignoring Church teaching or twisting it to justify whatever they want, and I see priests and other Church leaders causing scandals. It is a struggle sometimes for me to go to Mass because of the anger or disappointment I feel, or because of the lack of witnesses of what we teach and preach as Catholics. But I still hold on to what I know, from my conversion, from my reading, and from my four years of philosophy classes, and that is how I stay Catholic. There is also the lived experience of my Tia Mary's faith.

My Tia Mary was the kind of person who would bathe you in holy water if you came to her with problems and told her you were not baptized. If you were baptized, she would pray over you in front of her giant painting of Our Lady. Then there is my mother. My mom somehow found a statue of Mary that came with candleholders and has spent years and years lighting candles on it for me. Even when I was at my worst. When I was going to RCIA, I told my mom about the *Catechism* because I was shocked that all the teachings were written down. I thought that catechism was just a class that kids went to after school; I did not realize that the Church had put all its teachings together in a book so I bought one for my mom. She still has it next to her bed.

Neither of these women had any formal theology training, and yet both of them knew that when they needed something they could turn to Mary. They were the best theology teachers that I ever had.

After I became Catholic, I learned the story of the Rosary and began to try to pray it. I had rosary cards to remind me of the prayers, I had books on the Rosary, and I had tons of rosaries. To this day, I find rosaries in every single box of stuff from our move.

The two rosaries I have that mean the most to me are my St. Benedict medal rosary and one from Jen Fulwiler made from the roses that were on Anthony's coffin. I prayed the St. Benedict medal rosary with my Tia while my Tio was dying. (It was a super proud moment for me because I had a rosary in my purse and none of my cousins had theirs, so I got extra points.) My Tia led us in the most love-filled Rosary that I had ever heard in my life. Every Hail Mary and every Our Father was prayed with trust that God was hearing it. We no longer had any hope that my Tio was going to come out of his illness alive; we all knew that he was dying. So praying next to his bedside was an act of faith. It was also an act of love. When she could have been feeling sorry for herself or having anxiety and fear, instead my Tia turned to Mary. She taught me and my cousins to do the same. So when it was her lying in the bed dying ten months later, that is what we did.

My Tia's family has a tradition of praying a Rosary novena after someone dies. The first day of the novena is the day of their funeral. After my Tia's funeral, we all met at her house and prayed the first Rosary for her. Anthony was there, and he got a rosary from my car and sat down to pray it with us. A month later, I was sitting in front of his casket as a deacon led us in the Rosary after his suicide. Each time, I used my St. Benedict medal rosary. Each time the grief of the last Rosary carried over.

You would think that I am a champ at praying the Rosary and that I pray it every day, but that is not true. I am a mess and do not have my life together, which means I do not pray the Rosary like my Tia did. But here's the thing: the Rosary is important to me. Even if I do not bust it out every day and pray it, I carry it with me and I carry the lessons my Tia Mary taught me about love, life, and trusting that Our Lady is my mother.

When I do pray the Rosary, I don't always finish it. I let my angel finish my Rosary for me if I start it and fall asleep. That is something I heard about once, and I named it the "Loser Way to Pray the Rosary." More than anything, I no longer think that the Rosary is witchcraft or magic, but an act of trust and love. It's maybe especially an act of trust and love when I hand it off to my angel to finish for me. To know that the mother of Jesus takes my prayers and concerns to her Son gives me hope. It gives me peace, and it helps me to know that I am not alone.

I miss my Tio, Tia, and Anthony so much, and I only miss them more each passing day. I am so lucky to have had them in my life and to have learned the things they taught me. I am so lucky to have lived the life I've lived so that when I say that I believe God is good, I know it. I do not think God is good because my entire life has been good. I know he is good because he has given me great people to love and who love me—including his own mother. She does love me, even if I suck at praying the Rosary.

The thing I love the most about being Catholic is that I have found a place that hasn't gotten tired of my questions. I can ask them without fear of being kicked out. Having a relationship with God and with his mother does not mean that I know everything. It does not mean that I do not question why things are the way they are. But it does mean that I get to show up as me, even if that means that I fall asleep when I try to pray my Rosary at bedtime.

My husband and I were married on the Feast of Our Lady of the Rosary, and my son is buried in the Our Lady of the Rosary cemetery. Mary has always been watching over me, and she still is. This is something I have to remind myself when I feel inferior to the people I see on Instagram with their families praying the daily Rosary: Our Lady is not a scorekeeper. She loves us all. She doesn't help only those who check off boxes, but all of us. I am just as precious to her as the people who have their lives together enough to pray a daily Rosary, and knowing her love for me, I can stop comparing myself to them and anyone else.

I also consider that Hail Marys are what make up the Rosary and each one is a rose laid at her feet. So when I don't have time to pray the Rosary, I just try to lay spiritual roses at her feet like not cussing out a coworker or not flipping off someone in traffic or paying for someone's lunch. Those are all just as valid as roses to her. And that, my friends, is how to pray the Rosary like a loser when you do not have your life together. You just try not to be a jerk to others, and you think about those moments as roses laid at the feet of Our Lady. And you know that you are loved.

# ACKNOWLEDGMENTS

I do not know where to begin with acknowledging all the people who have helped me in my life. But I will begin with my mother, who raised me through her struggles and always made sure that I had home-cooked food and a clean house along with everything else I needed. She also made sure I had a lot of things I asked for, such as my own phone line with one of those phones that lit up when it rang. I thanked her by using it to call long distance and creating a huge phone bill she had to figure out how to pay. My mother also co-raised my children with me while I worked. I have never thanked her enough for my life and teaching me how to be fearless. I hope this covers a little of what I owe her.

Then there is my mentor, Tammy Shaklee. Thank you for encouraging me to make my big dreams come true—like writing, speaking, and graduating from college.

Thank you to my priests, Frs. Jonathan Raia and Dean Wilhelm. Both of them walked with me during the best days and worst days of my life. Because of their fatherhood, I have been able to slowly believe that God loves me.

Thank you to Noe Rocha. I only have five hundred words and I am writing this in public, so I can't express everything here, but Noe introduced me to Jesus and for that, I will forever be grateful.

Thank you to everyone—including my editor, who had to deal with me and my crazy—who has supported me and my writing for the last fifteen years. Thank you to Elizabeth Scalia, who hired me for my first writing gig, and the many writers who helped me along the way. Thank you to Jen Fulwiler for giving me space to be myself but also never acting as if I was not self-sabotaging my life when I was.

Thank you to Michelle Browning, the best freakin' therapist in the world. This book would be so different without her.

Stacey Wayne Adams, thank you for being my husband and making up for the heartbreak of being a jerk to me when we were kids. I love you to the moon and back.

Lastly, Anthony, my ride or die. He was the child who made me a mom, who dreamt big dreams with me, and whose encouragement and cheering I miss the most on days when my dreams come true because they were our dreams. I wish you were here. For all my other children who lost a lot of things so that I could figure out how to start a blog, social media platform, and all the things that come with this modern writing life, I want nothing more than to make it up to you.

If I forgot anyone, please forgive me. It took a lot of priests, friends, mentors and strangers from the internet to get this little book done. I hope y'all liked it, and if not, then I hope you bought it anyway so I can get electricity on the land. Thank you!

# NOTES

1. See, for example, Donna Jackson Nakazawa, *Childhood Disrupted: How Your Biography Becomes Your Biology, and How You Can Heal* (New York: Atria Books, 2015).

2. *Madea Goes to Jail*, directed by Tyler Perry (Lionsgate Films, 2009), DVD.

3. If you also struggle with this, put this book down and go buy Elizabeth Scalia's book, read it, and then come back. Seriously.

**Leticia Ochoa Adams** is a Catholic writer and speaker.

Since the death of her son, Anthony, by suicide in 2017, she has focused her work on being a witness to suffering and God's healing. Ochoa Adams is a contributor to several books, including *Surprised by Life*, *The Catholic Hipster Handbook*, *The Ave Prayer Book for Catholic Mothers*, and *Responding to Suicide*.

She has a bachelor's degree in philosophy from Holy Apostles College and Seminary. She has written for *Our Sunday Visitor*, *The National Catholic Reporter*, *FemCatholic*, *The Catholic Herald*, *Patheos*, and *Aleteia*. Ochoa Adams was a frequent guest on *The Jen Fulwiler Show* on SiriusXM's The Catholic Channel, and has appeared on a number of podcasts, including *Terrible, Thanks for Asking* with Nora McInerny.

She lives with her family in the Austin, Texas area.

leticiaoadams.com
**Facebook:** LeticiaOAdamsWriter
**Instagram:** @leticiaoadams

**Nora McInerny** is the author of *It's Okay to Laugh (Crying Is Cool Too)* and the host of the podcast *Terrible, Thanks for Asking*.

## AVE
### AVE MARIA PRESS

Founded in 1865, Ave Maria Press,
a ministry of the Congregation of
Holy Cross, is a Catholic publishing
company that serves the spiritual and
formative needs of the Church and its
schools, institutions, and ministers;
Christian individuals and families; and
others seeking spiritual nourishment.

For a complete listing of titles from

Ave Maria Press

Sorin Books

Forest of Peace

Christian Classics

visit avemariapress.com